A CLASS
OF THEIR OWN

A CLASS
OF THEIR OWN

Adventures in tutoring
the super-rich

by Matt Knott

First published in Great Britain in 2022 by Trapeze,
an imprint of The Orion Publishing Group Ltd
Carmelite House, 50 Victoria Embankment
London EC4Y 0DZ

An Hachette UK Company

1 3 5 7 9 10 8 6 4 2

A CIP catalogue record for this book is
available from the British Library.

ISBN (Hardback) 978 1 3987 0189 2
ISBN (eBook) 978 1 3987 0191 5
ISBN (Audio) 978 1 3987 0721 4

Typeset by Born Group
Printed and bound in Great Britain by Clays Ltd, Elcograf S.p.A.

www.orionbooks.co.uk

For my parents,
and real teachers everywhere

CONTENTS

DISCLAIMER

To respect the privacy of the families I worked with, I have altered various personal details. Despite these changes, the wealth and behaviour on display in these pages is an entirely authentic representation of the world I encountered during my career as a private tutor. I'm only sorry I couldn't use their real names. Seriously, you wouldn't believe what some of these people call their children.

PROLOGUE

A naked Russian oligarch is spanking me in his basement. His weapon is a birch branch, the setting his luxurious home sauna. Above us is 30,000 square feet of one of Moscow's most obscene private homes, an original Damien Hirst above the fireplace, a vacuum cleaning system built into the skirting boards. Risking great cultural offence, I have declined to remove my trunks on account of my twelve-year-old pupil Nikita — the oligarch's son — who sits beside me on a cedar bench, watching his father spank me. We are wearing pointy felt caps to keep our heads cool, causing the oligarch to resemble a kinky elf. Invisible speakers serenade us with a desolate pan pipe cover of 'Bridge Over Troubled Water'. A light display rotates kaleidoscopically, illuminating the oligarch's genitals in a variety of unexpected hues. Everyone is silent, but I can't think of anything to say that wouldn't make things worse. Then Nikita looks at me with a mysterious smile.

'Now my mother will bring us honey.'

Honey? Russian saunas are strictly gender segregated, but I should have known Nikita's mother Maria would

1

find a way in. I can't claim I hadn't encouraged her, having only days earlier serenaded her with a series of melodramatic love ballads at famed Moscow karaoke joint Who Is Who. On our chauffeured car ride home, she had fallen drunkenly asleep with her head in my lap and proceeded to have an intense dream while murmuring and licking her lips.

'Do you like it?' asks the oligarch, landing another strike on my thighs with his branch. I'm not sure if he means the honey or the spanking.

'Mmm,' I say non-committally.

While I have no desire to offend my host, I am equally keen for the experience to end. Not for the first time, I find myself wondering: how the hell did I end up here?

YEAR ONE

AUTUMN TERM 2008

Monday, 15 September, Dorset

It isn't every day the world falls apart before breakfast. As I got back from taking the dog for her morning walk, my parents were in the kitchen listening to Radio 4. Lehman Brothers had declared bankruptcy overnight. My mum looked up with a grave expression.

'Did Beanie do a poo on her walk?'

'Yes,' I said. 'But then she ate it.'

My mum rolled her eyes at my dad. Walking the dog had been my main responsibility since moving home a few weeks earlier. I had graduated from university in June, then starred in an original musical which debuted to half-full audiences and lukewarm reviews at the Edinburgh Fringe. Thanks to a four year course and a September birthday, I had somehow reached the practically geriatric age of twenty-three. My parents had made it clear that while I was forever welcome in the family home, it was time to become an adult and get a job.

'They're saying this could crash the world economy,' said my dad.

'What a time to be looking for a job,' said my mum pointedly.

'*Gone with the Wind* came out of the Great Depression,' I offered.

My parents exchanged another glance. It was no secret that I wanted to become a writer. I had dreamed of it since childhood, and had perfected an Oscar acceptance speech with the potential to reduce a global audience of millions to tears.

'It's not going to be handed to you on a plate,' said my mum.

She was right. In an ideal scenario, it would be handed to me by Jane Fonda.

I was all too aware that many of my contemporaries had stepped straight into well-paid careers in finance and management consultancy. But my own masterplan could not be said to be at an advanced stage. Earlier that week I'd had an idea for a script — a heartwarming comedy set in the fictional town of Piddle Newton. Now all I had to do was write it and let the acclaim roll in. My parents had always been very supportive of this plan, but they were eager for me to think about how I was going to support myself while I did it. Edinburgh had cleaned me out, and my NatWest savings account had been thin on good news ever since luring me with a free Young Persons Railcard.

'Why don't you see if the kitchens have any work?' said my dad for what felt like the sixth time that week.

He was referring to the catering company at the boarding school where he and my mum both taught, and where I had worked as a waiter every holiday throughout sixth form and university. Thanks to a generous staff bursary, I had also attended the school as a pupil. Aside from the obvious issues of being a student at the school where your parents taught, it also meant I had spent my teenage years surrounded by people with more money than me. When they jetted off to Barbados or Chamonix each Christmas and Easter, I clipped on a cheap bow tie and poured champagne at weddings for £4 an hour. When my swimming team turned up at a state school for a match and a teammate wondered if we were going to get stabbed, I cringed — until I turned twelve, I had attended my local primary school, where the worst thing I'd witnessed was my classmates on free school meals forced to line up in a separate lunch queue and get teased for wearing second-hand shoes. At that school, going camping in France or Cornwall had meant I was posh. But moving to private school, I was suddenly embarrassed to tell my French class what I did on my holidays when they had all stayed in villas or chalets and I had been slumming it in a tent.

Teenagers aren't known for their sense of perspective. I might have spent my days reciting Latin verbs while wearing a tweed jacket at a school which had its own golf course, but throughout my adolescence I thought

7

the fact that I had a holiday job meant I was basically Cinderella. Once I got to university in Cambridge and learned the phrase 'town versus gown', I realised that the supermarket checkout lady probably didn't care that I had gone to private school *on a scholarship*. But the damage had been done — a minor victim complex, and a lifelong insecurity around rich people. This wouldn't have been a problem if I had managed to steer well clear of them. I certainly had no intention of following my parents into what amounted to the family profession. My dad, a keen genealogist, had traced the ancestral line of teachers back eleven generations to a schoolmaster in Woking in 1672. Teaching was in my blood. But it had never been part of my life plan until later that day, when I texted my friend Zoe.

Me:	My parents are trying to make me become a scullery maid
Zoe:	Did you tell them you are in fact a literary genius?
Me:	THANK YOU. So tired of being undiscovered.
Zoe:	Come to London!
Me:	I can't afford it
Zoe:	Why don't you become a tutor? They always need more people. I'm making £30 an hour for helping kids do their homework.
Me:	WHAT?!

Zoe: You can stay on my sofa. Do you have any
            tutoring experience?
Me: Literally none
Zoe: We'll think of something

Tuesday, 23 September, Hammersmith

'Tell me about teaching in Guatemala,' Philippa said.

She peered at me with suspicion. Philippa was a stern woman in her forties who looked delighted to be back in a structured blazer after a summer of blouses. I had been surprised by how fast she had taken up Zoe's recommendation and invited me to an interview in her West London office. Now I was regretting putting the words 'TEACHER' and 'GUATEMALA' on my CV in quite such large font. On my year abroad for my Spanish degree, I had done a few weeks' volunteering at a school run by an alcoholic American man whose claim to fame was having once broken both his arms playing squash against himself. He had ended up in charge of a primary school in Guatemala, though it wasn't clear if he remembered how. My so-called drama classes had largely consisted of a few chaotic and occasionally violent rounds of Duck, Duck, Goose. I was suddenly aware that Philippa had been looking at me for quite a long time.

9

'They taught me as much as I taught them!' I said brightly.

Philippa nodded and cast a withering glance at my shoes. It was the second time I'd caught her doing it. Had I stepped in something? It would be tricky to check, though perhaps if I leaned forward I could get a sense of the general odour. But what would I do if I did detect a whiff? This was technically my first ever job interview, as the only question I recalled the catering company asking sixteen-year-old me was how I had managed to put on my bow tie back to front.

'Don't worry about your experience,' said Philippa. 'You went to Cambridge. Clients love that. It's more about making sure you . . . fit into their lifestyle.'

Suddenly I knew what the issue was with my Primark loafers. They were loafers from Primark. It was the same feeling I'd had when I first moved to private school and discovered that everyone wore the kind of high-end surf brands that were beyond my family's budget. I had trawled the racks at TK Maxx until I found a passable knock-off, but could still picture a boy decked in Quiksilver laughing as he asked if it was fake. From then on, I tended to make friends with other scholarship kids. This worked well enough until my first black tie 18th, where I was the only guest who failed to get the host a gift. 'Don't drink it all at once!' I scrawled in my card, before propping it in among the bottles of Bollinger and Veuve Clicquot. By the time I got to Cambridge, I was sophisticated enough to buy the hummus with a scattering of whole chickpeas when I was hosting pre-drinks. But I don't think I had ever shaken the fear that I might be found out at any moment. I wondered how to explain this to Philippa without sounding self-indulgent, and whether it would be overly dramatic to compare myself to that scene in *The Great Escape* where the British soldier gets caught because he can't help thanking someone in English when they wish him good luck.

'That won't be a problem,' I said.

'Excellent,' said Philippa. 'As long as you don't have any skeletons in your closet.'

It was an unfortunate choice of words. Fitting in at school hadn't only been a question of keeping up with the Joneses. I had also hidden the fact that I was very, very gay. Philippa had made it clear that she was hiring me because I fitted a certain profile which made me an easy sell to her client base. Anything which complicated that picture, I decided to keep to myself — for now.

Philippa explained that due to my limited experience she would start me off as a 'study buddy' — a comfortingly juvenile-sounding role focused on revision and homework help.

'This is a bit cheeky,' said Philippa, 'but one of our tutors has food poisoning. How do you feel about jumping straight in?'

Mum: That's great! When do you start?
Me: NOW

11

Tuesday, 23 September, Mayfair

There was something uncannily familiar about being sent to teach in Mayfair. Then I realised it was the Monopoly board. But far from being able to purchase the entire area for £400 after tricking my brother into paying over the odds for Pall Mall, a quick google told me that the average house price here was £2 million. Properties on the square where I was heading went for four or five times that. As I walked along the tree-lined street in shoes I had hastily attempted to polish with a Kleenex, I started to sweat. But ever since witnessing a then unknown Darren Day seize his moment while deputising for Phillip Schofield in a production of *Joseph and the Amazing Technicolor Dreamcoat* at the London Palladium, I had known that dazzling as an understudy could be the first step on the path to greatness.

By the time I arrived at the address, I was really putting my Right Guard Total Defence deodorant to the test. The house was on the same square as the imperious American embassy, adding to the sense of grandeur and formality. I was no more prepared to teach a lesson than I was to meet the ambassador to Cameroon over a tricky diplomatic incident. At least Darren Day got a dress rehearsal. As I approached the towering stucco terrace, I noticed a bodyguard on duty two doors down. I walked up to the front door and rang the bell. A security camera blinked on and an accented voice crackled over the intercom.

'Come to the muse.'

'Sorry, where?'

'The muse. Round the back.'

I suddenly worried I had got the wrong address and stumbled into some sort of *Eyes Wide Shut*-style sex party, and that The Muse would turn out to be a Conservative Cabinet minister in a gimp mask. But as I hurried to the rear of the house, I realised my mistake. *The mews.* Each house was backed by a corresponding mews cottage, which in my case had been helpfully marked 'Tradesman's Entrance'. On any other day that would have gone straight on Facebook with a cheeky caption, but I had never felt less like a man with a trade. Before I could ring the bell for a second time, the door swung open and I was greeted by a petite woman with a bowl haircut and a blank expression.

'Hi, I'm—'

'Feet!'

The woman pointed to a small cardboard box on the floor, the logic between her statement and the gesture not immediately apparent. I examined the box and saw that it appeared to contain shower caps. Then I realised they were supposed to be placed over my shoes as a kind of foot condom.

'Quick!' the woman urged. No sooner had I pulled on the foot condoms than she led me off through a side door and down a set of stairs into the basement. We passed an underground swimming pool sparkling beneath a skylight, then the woman — still nameless

13

— stopped and pressed a button. The wall slid open, revealing a lift.

'Wait upstairs,' she said, bundling me in.

As the door glided shut and the lift ascended, I was half expecting to emerge into the gimp mask sex ceremony. I stepped out into a vast entrance hall. The white walls and polished surfaces felt like a comment on my own unforgivably scuffed appearance, and I knew I was going to somehow smash a vase or soil the carpet. I noticed I was metres away from the main door I had been banned from entering. Then I realised I was not alone.

Seated on the stairs, leaning back on his elbows, was a man about my age. He was handsome, dressed in cords and a polo shirt, and brimming with the kind of casual swagger that reminded me of the boys I'd gone to school with. It wasn't really their money I'd envied in my teens. It was the way their lives seemed to unfold with such *ease* — socially confident and permanently refreshed from an endless cycle of foreign holidays while I stayed locked in my bedroom applying Clearasil Complete and cursing the fact that I had crushes on all of them.

I was suddenly very self-conscious about what to do with my hands. I knew immediately that this guy was a tutor, but a proper one, against whom even the slightest comparison would expose me as a fraud. In that way that comes so naturally to the English, we shared a glance then studiously ignored each other. A few moments later, the petite woman returned. Behind her was *another tutor*.

14

What the hell was happening? Presumably the family used multiple tutors, but surely it wasn't necessary to gather us in a holding pen. I had once temped in an office where I had been assigned the email account Assistant2, with another for the more senior Assistant1. There was no need for either of us to have individual identities, since we would soon be rotated out and replaced with a new assistant. In a similar spirit, I decided these other tutors would be known as Tutor1 and Tutor2. The woman approached Tutor1.

'Can you do Emil today, Nick?'

'Excuse me,' I wanted to say. 'His *name* is Tutor1.' I had been comforted by the thought that we were all anonymous. But not only was this so-called 'Nick' on first-name terms, he had been picked ahead of me. I still wasn't sure if these counted as rational reasons to resent him.

The woman turned to Tutor2.

'And you do Roman?'

At least she appeared to agree there was no need to know Tutor2's name. Tutor2 nodded, giving no indication he had any idea who Roman was. Finally the woman turned to me.

'Thanks,' she said. 'We don't need you today.'

Mum: How did it go?
Me: It didn't

15

Wednesday, 24 September, Mayfair

It couldn't be claimed I had taught my first lesson poorly. 'It happens,' said Philippa when I called in a panic. 'You'll still get paid.'

Paid for *that?* I was convinced it was a kill fee. Was this because I hadn't known what a mews was? I splashed out on some shoe polish and resisted the urge to call my parents. But the very next day, I was asked back. Maybe I'd got this all wrong. If I was only a backup tutor, as appeared to be the case, I could slip on my condom socks and ride it out without ever teaching a lesson. I silently wished the tutor with food poisoning a long and drawn-out recovery.

In the entrance hall, Nick was nowhere to be seen but Tutor2 was waiting along with a new Tutor1. My naming system had proved its worth already. It felt rude to extend this policy to the woman who ran things round here, but she told me her name was Nadia with such a disparaging look that I sensed trading personal details was the mark of an amateur.

'You've got Roman today,' said Nadia to Tutor1.

This made no sense — Roman had been assigned to Tutor2 last time. Nadia turned to me. 'And you're with Emil.'

Damn. I was going to have to teach. Nadia looked at Tutor2. 'That means you've got Samir.'

Samir? So there was a third child.

Nadia led us upstairs. Tutor1 and Tutor2 appeared to know exactly where they were going, splitting off without a word. On the top floor, we arrived at a bedroom. Seated at a desk was a boy with enormous brown eyes which gazed at me with a mixture of curiosity and suspicion. Nadia had told me on our way up that Emil was five, but I had pictured someone older and couldn't believe this tiny child was going to be left in my care. 'Sorry,' I wanted to say to Nadia. 'I think there's been a mistake. Have you *seen* my CV?'

Nadia gave me an ominous look. 'Watch out. He's just been circumcised.'

Just been circumcised? How recently are we talking? Watch out for *what*? But Nadia had vanished. I stepped into the room.

'Do you have a willy?' said Emil.

I stared at him.

'For that you must go to hospital. It's very bad.'

'I'm here to help you do your homework,' I said, blushing.

To my relief I noticed that someone had already laid it out on the desk.

'Come on,' I said. 'Which pen do you want to use?'

'This one!' said Emil, seizing a pair of scissors and lunging towards me.

'No!' I cried, wrestling the scissors off him.

Emil ceded his weapon and examined me calmly.

'Can I put a sticker on your willy?'

I hesitated, though not because I was considering his proposition. I was worried that anything I said could be used against me in court. But maybe that was preferable to a revenge circumcision. Before I could decide whether to hand myself in to the police or take my chances jumping out of the window, Emil announced that he needed the loo. He went across the landing to the bathroom and I breathed a sigh of relief. But five minutes later he still hadn't emerged. I stepped onto the landing.

'Emil? Are you OK?'

'Come in!'

I couldn't say I was gagging to enter a toilet containing a five-year-old. But my mind was playing out various catastrophic outcomes if I didn't. Emil was on the floor on all fours, his pants round his ankles, his bum pointing at me. He looked up hopefully.

'Will you swish my bottom?'

Me: Are you free tonight? It's an emergency
Zoe: See you at 8

Wednesday, 24 September, Holloway Road

Until I had a success to show off about — a BAFTA nomination, or at the very least a writing credit on *Holby City* — I planned to keep my move to London relatively quiet. The only dignified stance was a faint air of mystery. This was confirmed by my fellow graduates, who were either posting entire Facebook albums of themselves doing shots at Mahiki after a twenty-two-hour day at Merrill

Lynch, or daily video diaries which became increasingly unhinged as they toured a bold new adaptation of *Hedda Gabler* around the Balkans. Rather than accept Zoe's offer of a sofa, I had taken the plunge and rented a room in a flat share with two strangers — a straight couple with identical mullets who worked in admin but had a start-up business selling highly amusing T-shirts. NatWest had extended my student overdraft for a year to cover the deposit, and while I didn't like living on money that wasn't real, I was sure it was temporary. The couple had so far shown great tolerance towards my laissez-faire approach to kitchen hygiene. But tonight, my panicked emotional state coupled with my poor culinary skills had turned the place into a bomb site.

Zoe was the type of small-framed woman who gets described as a firecracker, as if she were expected to have all the personality of Polly Pocket. I had always admired her ability to pull on a jumper and trainers and be the most stylish person in the room — not that competition was fierce on this occasion.

'What are you cooking?' she asked with a note of not-quite-concealed trepidation.

It was a good question. I had gone to the supermarket with the intention of buying the ingredients for spaghetti bolognese, but had been distracted by an offer on my favourite lunch item. Now I had twenty-four cans of bean soup and a pasta sauce unlikely to pass quality control at Pedigree Chum. Zoe had contributed a bottle of our favourite Tesco Soave — a wine so watery that for £5 it didn't taste bad, nor really of anything at all. I decanted almost the entire bottle between two glasses then began gulping mine down.

'It was fun while it lasted,' I said between gulps. 'I just hope I get fired and not arrested.'

'I thought you said you didn't wipe his bum.'

'Of course I didn't! Wait, was that wrong?'

'God no,' said Zoe. 'That was a test.'

'You think he was testing me?'

'Five-year-olds know how to wipe their own bums.'

'But surely no tutor would agree to do that?'

'Maybe that's why he gets through so many. He still hasn't found The One.'

For the first time all day, I smiled. It was precisely for this kind of breezy reassurance I had invited Zoe round. She had been tutoring for a year now while she tried to build her portfolio as a graphic designer, and took situations like this in her stride.

'It's all just so *weird*,' I said. 'Where are the parents?'

'Fuck knows. Ascot. Harrods. Dubai.'

'I can't believe they don't care who's teaching their sons. They're paying me thirty pounds an hour.'

'That's *nothing* to them.'

'We're in a recession!'

'We are. They're not.'

At school in Dorset, being rich meant a swimming pool in the garden or a Jaguar in the garage. But I was starting to realise I had only seen the half of it. Zoe admitted she had been expecting the work to dry up or at least slow down ever since the economy started crumbling. But for the type of client who paid for homework help, it appeared to be business as usual.

'You can't call this teaching,' I said.

'God no. It's posh babysitting.'

I presume I betrayed a glimmer of disillusion.

'If you want to do something useful, you can fundraise for Save the Children.'

'Wouldn't I earn like four times less?'

'Well, yeah. And eat way more bean soup.'

I felt obliged to go on an impassioned rant about the miracle that was a 45p can of protein and complex carbohydrate. But it had occurred to me there were worthier ways to earn money. Then again, this wasn't a vocation. It was the easiest way to finance my writing career.

'Don't overthink it,' Zoe advised. 'But get some more clients. You don't want all your eggs in one basket.'

NEW JOB ALERT

Job number: 3062

Subject: Literacy skills

What: Monty's recent test scores have not been up to scratch. His parents want to take a holistic approach by encouraging a love of reading in the mornings before school.

Where: Chelsea

When: Monday, Wednesday and Friday, 8–9 a.m.

They sound bonkers! Ask if he's done Toe by Toe –
it's a structured programme which is supposed to be
good at boosting reading age. I'll look up some stuff
and call you this evening. You'll need lots of variety
– you can't possibly read for that long.

Mum x

Monday, 6 October, Chelsea

Philippa had warned it might take a while to build up a
client list, but I guessed other tutors had balked at the
early start time. Personally I was thrilled at the thought
of lessons at 8 a.m.: a morning commute surely made me
an adult with a real job. On a sunny autumn day like
this, it was hard to imagine a more wholesome activity
than reading. I might not be saving the world, but maybe
I would inspire the next E. M. Forster. I trudged from
the Tube laden down with a rucksack full of books. In
theory, having a special needs expert as a parent was an
invaluable resource. In practice, I listened to my mum
talk authoritatively about phonics, then promptly spent
the weekend focusing on which books would get a child
to like me, while also convincing his parents I was the
kind of erudite young gentleman they should keep on
their payroll. This led to an over-enthusiastic smash and
grab on a charity shop which left me with such a random
and extensive bibliography that I was better equipped

22

to operate a mobile library in rural Wiltshire than put together a coherent reading programme for a child.

My customary google had revealed that the average house price in Chelsea was a mere £1.5 million. However, as I arrived at a row of imposingly large townhouses, I realised this was no average home. The next door property was a building site, workmen cranking into action even at this hour. But not only was I allowed in by the front door this time, I was greeted by a parent. Charles, my pupil's father, was round and red-faced, though it was too early to say whether it was rosacea, alcoholism or sunburn from a week in Santorini. As he showed me in, I almost tripped over a lacrosse stick, so artfully placed that this could have been the set of a Farrow & Ball catalogue shoot. There was a dusty smell, possibly due to a mouldy old rug which I imagined some racist great uncle had got his manservant to ship over from colonial Burma. There was no question – I was in the presence of old money.

'So,' said Charles, preceding the traditional 'o' sound with a nasal 'e' that the word's spelling in no way suggested. 'Biggles.'

'Biggles?' I said. I was pretty sure I had heard him correctly, but without any context it could have been anything from a niche upper class greeting to a nick-name for his child.

'Biggles,' Charles said proudly, which was the maximum number of times two people could reasonably repeat the word at each other outside of an absurdist theatre piece. 'That's the plan.'

Before I could respond, Charles's wife Gwen emerged. She was wearing riding boots, and I wanted to ask if this was the latest fashion or she was planning to drive out to Surrey after breakfast and mount a horse. There was no reason not to think that the first and perhaps only thing she was planning to say to me was 'Biggles'.

'Sorry about next door,' Gwen said. 'Russians.'

She cast a sorrowful glance at her husband.

'Have you *seen* the crack in this wall?'

I was fairly sure that not only had Charles seen it, but that Gwen took delight in pointing it out whenever anyone visited. For all I knew, it had actually been caused by one of her own children after a particularly bad loss at lacrosse.

'Can I offer you a smoothie?' she said. 'I like to add my own twist.'

I accepted Gwen's offer, leaving Charles to elaborate on what was clearly a subject dear to his heart. Biggles, it turned out, was the title character of a novel series about a fighter pilot. Charles had consumed the books voraciously as a child and was determined to light a similar spark in his son Monty.

'God I loved Biggles,' Charles said wistfully, as though he and the fictional pilot had conducted a torrid affair during the Battle of the Somme. Gwen returned with my smoothie, which I dutifully sipped. Unless I was missing something, her big gastronomic innovation was a mild amount of ginger.

'She smuggles it into everything,' Charles said proudly.

Gwen gave him one of those sly marital grins which made me wonder if she occasionally spiced things up in the bedroom by sliding a piece up his bum. It was time to meet Monty. He was eight, and resembled one of those characters Enid Blyton rather gleefully condemns for having eaten too many boiled sweets.

'Right then, Monty,' said Charles. 'Biggles.'

The man needed gagging, or quite possibly a course of therapy, but eventually he left us to it. Once again, I couldn't help be astonished and mildly offended at the lack of interest in *me*. I had crafted a series of elegant answers to any questions I might get asked, which I hoped would pitch me as the kind of charming but unthreatening friend of the family who could be trusted to make themselves a cheese sandwich. But Gwen and Charles didn't show even an ounce of curiosity.

'Do I *have* to read?' said Monty.

I suggested that his father would be very disappointed if he didn't.

'OK fine, but in my head.'

Monty began to read in silence. At least I presume that's what he was doing — there was no way for me to know he wasn't thinking about SpongeBob SquarePants. Surely Charles and Gwen weren't paying me to sit there doing nothing? Then again, it wasn't clear why they were paying me to read with their son in the first place, rather than doing it themselves. I told Monty he had to read at least some of the book out loud, but he rapidly negotiated me down to dialogue only. For a few paragraphs, he was quiet. Then he looked up.

'It's me, Dickpa!'

I almost choked on my smoothie.

'Pardon?'

Dickpa, to my relief, was Biggles' name for his uncle. Posh people loved nothing better than a nickname with a faint air of smut. As Monty continued to read, randomly interjecting bursts of dialogue between Biggles and Dickpa, I noticed a second Biggles adventure lying on the table. Flicking to the back, I was horrified to learn that the series ran to a comprehensive ninety-eight volumes. There was more than a faint air of smut to titles like 'Biggles Gets His Men' and 'Biggles Takes It Rough'. But as Monty read on, the text offered nothing more than bland military jingoism. This wasn't just about improving Monty's reading skills. It was about passing down a literary inheritance from father to son, presumably as it had been handed down to Charles. I wondered if Charles's ancestors had been fighter pilots. Unlikely. They were far more likely to have been in high command, never closer to the battlefield than shifting models around a table.

Just then, Charles popped his head in, presumably because going more than ten minutes without saying the word 'Biggles' had serious medical implications.

'How are you finding it?'

'We're loving it!' I said.

'Smashing,' said Charles. 'You can read the whole series.'

TUTORING REPORT: MONTY CALVIN

What have you been working on?
Biggles

What form of assessment have you used to measure progress?
Biggles

What areas have seen improvement and what needs more work?
Biggles

What will you be working on next month?
Biggles

Monday, 3 November, Mayfair

Receiving my first pay cheque was very exciting. It was also a reality check. The hourly rate was far beyond what I had earned as a waiter. But since most clients only wanted an hour or two each week and the windows for tutoring were limited, I was a long way off piecing together a timetable that would cover the mounting costs of adulthood. I knew the worst case scenario for someone like me was moving back to Dorset with my tail between my legs. But I was determined it would never

27

come to that. Luckily I was good at making a little go a long way, perhaps because I had grown up with a pocket money book. My parents had set weekly pocket money as our age times 10p, at some point adding a 30p bonus to make the equation 10x + 30. Rather than count out the various permutations for four young children, they had bought us a notebook where you could write in your weekly, say, £1.10 (as I received aged eight) and watch it accumulate in time for the new Spice Girls cassette, while making judicious splashes on a packet of Skittles or a fortnightly copy of *Smash Hits*. Unfortunately it was hard to deny that times had changed.

'Don't forget to put some aside for tax,' said my mum when I called her.

This sounded like a good idea, but so did the Top Man sale — I needed some way to recover from the discovery that you had to pay for your own water. At least I was now a regular in the holding pen. When I arrived that day, Nick was in his previous position on the stairs. I planned to ignore him indefinitely, but he looked at me with a puzzled expression.

'Where do I know you from?' he said. 'Did you do National Youth Theatre?'

'No,' I wanted to thunder, 'I am entirely self-made. I mounted a full production of *Mary Poppins* at my state primary school, directing myself in the titular role. It caused a major schism with my good friend Katherine Brown, to whom I had promised the role of Poppins, but I regret nothing. The production was a roaring success.'

'*That*'s it,' Nick said. 'That Edinburgh show.'

Great. So he already saw me as a flop. Thankfully Nick was more interested in telling me about *his* Edinburgh show, which had just staged a transfer to a Soho theatre. I could barely conceive of mounting a professional production so soon after graduating, and hoped it had been a disaster.

'The critics were terribly kind, bless them,' Nick said.

I forced a smile and assumed they were all family friends.

Nadia appeared and escorted us to our stations. Nick had been assigned the middle child, Samir, while I had Roman, the eldest. He was ten, with a solemn demeanour, and had already cracked on with the maths exercise he had been set. Across the hall, I heard Nick start to dictate Samir's answers to him. Surely that's not what we were being paid to do? Roman appeared not to require any assistance, which felt like an equally strange thing to be paid for. Since I hadn't been set nightly homework when I was their age, I couldn't claim to be an expert.

'How do you do long division again?' asked Roman.

Shit. Long division was my Achilles' heel, my Waterloo, my Kryptonite. When people claim to understand it, I assume they are lying. Something about it sends my brain into retreat. What was wrong with me? I was the son of a maths teacher for god's sake. Then I realised that was the answer. I got out my phone under the table.

Me:	Are you there?
Dad:	I'm in a department meeting. Is something the matter?
Me:	Yes! My career is on the line

Taking a photo of the offending question, I sent it to my dad with no further explanation. I am not sure if he was engaged in a similarly furtive effort or got the whole maths team involved. But a few seconds later, he texted back the answer. I copied it out for Roman, passing it off as my own work. This wasn't cheating like Nick. It was a creative teaching method. How my dad arrived at the answer, I still have no idea.

Thursday, 13 November, Fulham

Reading the reviews for Nick's play was a bad idea. The critics were falling over themselves to anoint him The Next Big Thing. Perhaps they were not aware of my heartwarming comedy set in the fictional town of Piddle Newton? This was understandable, considering that I had not yet written it. I trusted that the muse would strike me soon, but first I had other priorities. Due to a perfect storm of budgetary constraints and an ongoing lack of anything to show off about, I had done very little socialising since moving to London. Even going to the pub with Zoe and her housemates became a trial in nursing a single gin and tonic for three hours, knowing that accepting any offers left me at risk of having to buy a round. Tonight, however, I had been invited to my first grown-up dinner party. The hostess was not a friend so much as a woman who had lived in my university halls and been a reliable source of Kettle Chips. But she had urged me to come, claiming there was someone she wanted me to meet. In honour of the occasion, I upgraded my regular Soave to a bottle of Tesco's Finest, which came in at an extravagant £6.99.

I couldn't understand how the hostess had such a nice flat — was she blowing her entire income on rent for the sake of appearances, or getting some help from the bank of mum and dad? It took about five minutes to recall why she was only an acquaintance. She breathlessly introduced me to my fellow guests, each one more objectionable than the last. They included a lawyer doing a training contract at a firm named after his grandfather, and a management consultant who kept loudly announcing that she had fucked a clown.

'It's actually a really competitive starting salary,' said the lawyer.

'He gave me the best head of my life,' said the management consultant.

I dreaded to think which of these nightmares the hostess had wanted me to meet. I was tempted to bolt, but she had taken it upon herself to slow-roast a ham and it felt rude to leave before dinner had been served.

'What do you do?' asked the woman who had fucked a clown.

Not that question. Tutoring was what I did, if barely, but that wouldn't cut it with a crowd like this. Was it worse to hide my writing ambitions or admit I'd done nothing towards them?

'I do rich kids' homework,' I said.

I was spared any further interrogation by the arrival of another guest — a good-looking Scottish man who blushed as he shook my hand. I wanted to tell him to run while he still could, but the clown fucker barely allowed him to take off his coat before asking the inevitable question.

'I'm a classroom assistant for kids with learning difficulties,' he revealed.

'Fantastic,' said the lawyer. 'Good man.'

'Joel and I did a musical together,' said the hostess, sensing that some additional information was required to understand how such a decent person had ended up anywhere near her. She grinned at me. 'I thought you guys might get on.'

Joel and I shared a glance as we realised what she had done. Nobody is more pleased with themselves than a straight person who has succeeded in assembling two or more gays in one room. Naturally we are always grateful, since it's not like we have come up with any way of doing this ourselves. Despite her satisfaction, I couldn't help feel our hostess had miscalculated badly. Sure, we were both fans of musical theatre. But if Joel was a good man, what was I?

Zoe: How was it?

Me: Full of twats. Plus this guy who helps kids with learning difficulties who made me feel really bad about tutoring.

Zoe: That's a bit much for a Friday night

Me: No, he didn't say anything. He was way too nice. And cute.

Zoe: You slept with him, didn't you

Friday, 14 November, Chelsea

After the effort our hostess had made, it would have been rude not to. Although given the amount of wine I drank, there wasn't really much sleeping of either variety. I wasn't even sure if I fancied Joel or just wanted to convince him I was a good person. Maybe it was me I was trying to convince. The more pressing issue was that I had woken up in Joel's flat in Kilburn with a brutal hangover and was due to teach Monty in an hour. Jumping on the Tube to Chelsea, I narrowly avoided vomiting into the bag of an elderly woman and sitting in the lap of a bodybuilder — or maybe it was the other way round; it's all a bit blurry. By the time Gwen opened the door to me, I was barely holding it together.

'You're one of those poofters, aren't you?' I was sure she was thinking. There was something about the domestic setting

33

which took me back to being a teenager and in the closet from my parents. I had made it through a whole term without the subject arising, and I was perfectly happy for it to stay that way. I was, after all, the great-grand-nephew of Mildred Knott, who worked as a PE teacher at a girls' school in the 1920s while quietly living with another woman. Then again, I doubt Mildred ever preceded a day of lessons by dry humping a classroom assistant in Kilburn.

'Would you like to try my latest smoothie combo?' Gwen smiled. 'Strawberry and banana.'

It was bold to claim invention of one of the most common of all fruit combinations, but I was grateful for the vitamin boost. As I sat down with Monty, I began to fear my ability to make it through the hour. There was a teepee on the other side of the room, and I tried in vain to think of a teaching exercise which involved me curling up inside it and having a nap. Monty reached for Biggles, but even the thought of it made me queasy. It wasn't the morning to be reading about the misadventures of two men in a cockpit.

'Let's read something else today,' I said.

I picked up a book that was clearly intended for five-year-olds.

'That's my brother's,' said Monty.

That didn't seem any reason not to read *Sid Did It!*. In fact, I was curious to know what Sid had done and why it had merited a whole book. As Monty started to read, I could sense his reluctance, but the childlike rhymes were right at my current intellectual level and far more palatable than Biggles' stodgy prose. I looked up to see Charles entering. I hurriedly swapped the book, thrusting our latest Biggles volume in front of Monty.

'How's the old rotter?' asked Charles.

'Great, yeah,' I said.

Charles had a furtive look about him, and you had to wonder how recently Gwen had performed his favourite trick with a knob of ginger.

'I got a rather funny voicemail from you at 3 a.m.' Charles said.

My heart stopped. Charles mumbled about not needing to worry and headed back out. I pulled out my phone and saw a missed call at the alleged time.

'Why did you call him?' Monty asked.

I vaguely recalled complaining to Joel about having to tutor in the morning, but couldn't imagine I had called Charles to cancel. This left the horrifying possibility that I had dialled him by accident. Charles hadn't acted as if I had broadcast anything inappropriate, but how could I be sure I hadn't sent him an exclusive recording of my two-star erotic encounter? I could never look him in the eye again.

Hi Philippa,
Would be great to get some more clients!
Not sure how much more Biggles I can handle.

Won't be any new clients now til January.
Been a long term. Hang in there.
    P

Tuesday, 2 December, Mayfair

Though I now knew and loathed Nick and recognised at least one other tutor, I couldn't keep track of all the staff that passed through the holding pen. I spotted everyone from a florist to a Luxury Mobile Dog Groomer (*sic*), dutifully putting on their plastic socks and heading underground. It was hard to believe we were all strictly necessary. We felt more like seat warmers, hired to make this cavernous space feel lived in while its owners were off god knows where. Nadia handled the whole pantomime with admirable poise. But today when I turned up, she was stressed.

'You've got Emil,' said Nadia. 'And can you give him his supper? It's in the kitchen.'

Before I could get any further instructions she rushed off, muttering something about motion sensor light bulbs. I had taught Emil, my five-year-old nemesis, a few times by now and had managed to avoid any bottom swishing, willy stickering or other career-ending incidents. I went up to his room and told him I was meant to be getting him his dinner.

'Where?' Emil said, scanning my hands with confusion as to why I wasn't presenting it to him on a gold tray.

'Apparently it's in the kitchen.'

Emil led me there hungrily. But there was no food in sight. The fridge was empty, the surfaces so devoid of any incriminating evidence that it could have been the scene of a murder cover-up.

'What do you normally eat?'

Emil opened a drawer and pulled out a menu. Takeaway had rarely been part of my childhood, though I'm not sure if it was because my mum thought it was unhealthy or too expensive for a family of six. I had spent the whole of 1997 trying without success to convince her that what we wanted for dinner was a KFC family bucket. But this wasn't a leaflet that had been posted through the letter box. It was a proper menu that looked like it had been personally provided by the restaurant in question. It listed dishes like lobster tempura and miso black cod which cost more for a single portion than my weekly supermarket shop.

'Is this really what you get for supper?'

Emil nodded. Not wanting to be held responsible for starving a child, I called up and ordered his request of noodles, paying on my card and figuring I'd settle with Nadia. In no time the noodles had been delivered and Emil was slurping them with relish. Then we heard the front door. Emil looked up in a panic.

'What?'

His guilty expression said it all.

'We weren't meant to do this, were we?'

Emil began slurping his noodles at double speed. The little shit. I could feel the fumes seeping into the curtains and carpet, and knew that if Nadia caught so much as a whiff I'd be fired on the spot. I opened the window, then looked at Emil. It was unfair to expect someone so small to destroy the evidence at such speed, not to mention bad for his digestion. It had absolutely nothing to do with exacting revenge on a five-year-old. I seized his dinner and swallowed it in one gulp. As I squashed the empty box into the bottom of my bag, Nadia appeared in the doorway.

'Why didn't you give him his supper?'

'I . . . the kitchen was empty.'

'Which kitchen did you check?'

Which kitchen. What a rookie error. My ignorance revealed, I figured I may as well clarify something that had been bugging me all term.

'So how many brothers are there?'

'Three.'

'And why do they sometimes have the right number of tutors and sometimes the wrong number?'

Nadia looked puzzled.

'They only need a tutor if they have homework.'

Finally the system was clear. Three tutors meant they were covered if everyone had homework. If not, one or more got sent home. I was struggling to think like a rich person. The cost wasn't relatively minor. It was not something they thought about at all.

CHRISTMAS

'I cannot believe you get paid for this,' said my brother.

'How *much* he gets paid,' my other brother chipped in.

'It's harder than it sounds,' I insisted.

'It's Biggles,' said my sister.

I was back in Dorset and gathered round the dinner table with my parents and siblings. My contribution to the meal was a bottle of wine Charles and Gwen had given me for Christmas along with a £100 tip. It was only when one of my brothers looked it up that we realised the wine was a vintage Chardonnay worth almost as much as the tip.

'Lucky you,' said my mum. 'The best I got from a pupil this year was a plastic figurine of the Beijing Olympic mascot.'

'Speak for yourself,' said my dad. 'I got a solid bronze replica model of the Flying Horse of Gansu.'

Needless to say, I wasn't among company where gifts from wealthy parents were any kind of novelty. But while my parents had no doubt earned their bounties, that wasn't the general consensus for my term's efforts.

'How can *you* tutor maths?' asked my brother.

'He can't,' said my dad.

'That was one time.'

'No it wasn't. Last week you had to ask me if product meant add or multiply.'

He wasn't wrong. But there had been no suggestion the client believed in the value of homework or cared how it got done. I pointed out that they had made no complaints.

'That's because you haven't met them,' said my brother. 'What if it's an arms dealer?'

'Then that arms dealer is inadvertently funding an Oscar-winning script.'

As I said it, I realised it wasn't quite the zinger I had hoped. Not wanting to dwell on my non-existent writing career, I conceded that the ethics of my chosen profession were not exemplary. But there was no use agonising over hypotheticals. For all I knew, the boys' parents were major philanthropists.

'Have the parents really not met you?' said my mum.

'Not once.'

She gave me a wry smile.

'No wonder it's going so well.'

On Christmas Day, we went to church in the local town. After the service, a stout man who had sent both his sons to my parents' school approached and asked what I had been up to since graduating. I responded with some quip about Biggles. The man looked appalled.

'So that's what a Cambridge degree gets you these days, is it?'

I gave him the laugh he was after, but he wasn't done yet.

'Daniel was very lucky to get a job at Linklaters,' he said. 'And Tom is loving his final year of law.'

He asked what my older brother was doing and seemed astonished to learn he was also freelancing.

'Wait,' he said, utterly giddy. 'So *neither* of you has a salary?'

He couldn't believe someone could have an education like mine at a time like this and not seek the comfort of a secure profession. Maybe he was onto something.

Once we got home, it was time to open our presents. This was a race to see who had given me some useless set of toiletries and who had honoured the Christmas spirit and supplied cold hard cash. One great aunt had stuck so consistently over the years to sending a fiver that I had gone from seeing it as the height of extravagance to wanting to send her a passive-aggressive thank you letter asking if she had heard of inflation. But my granny understood the deal. 'In my day this was a lot of money,' she wrote with her cheque. 'These days it will probably only get you a round of drinks.'

On Boxing Day we went for a walk round the grounds of the school where we lived. People often asked me what it was like growing up in a boarding school. In my childhood, when my dad was in charge of a house of sixty boys, I didn't think of the pupils as having things I didn't. I focused on the perks — stealing packets of Space Raiders from the kitchen store cupboards, or being allowed to eat the 'boys' tea' (chicken Kiev if I was lucky) on a Wednesday when I got home late from Cub Scouts. The holidays were the best part of living on campus. During term you shared the place with 600 pupils. Then they disappeared and the school was yours. When I was six, I had claimed in my news book that I had a tennis court and a football pitch 'in my garden', prompting frenzied enquiries from my teacher. As I got older, it was more like we'd been given free rein of Center Parcs. There was a Boxing Day tradition where staff and their children gathered on the Astroturf for a hockey match. I had retired following one or two unmemorable appearances in early adolescence, but they were out there again today, larking around on a pitch that was usually reserved for pupils paying tens of thousands of pounds a year for the privilege.

'Look, it's Jenny Francis,' said my mum. 'She's just started her PGCE.'

'I'm thinking of doing that,' said my sister. 'Eventually.'

'Nice to have another one in the family,' said my dad.

'A teacher?'

'A salary.'

CHRISTMAS

Me: Hey Joel – hope you're enjoying the break.
I'm going to be back in London next week.
Let me know if you want to hang out!

SPRING TERM 2009

Wednesday, 14 January, Highgate

I had no idea there were private roads in London. I had never even been to Highgate, but according to Google it was home to everyone from George Michael to Kate Moss. The road had a security barrier and a booth with a guard who demanded to know my purpose. As I passed the checkpoint, a woman with a spaniel gave me such a snotty look that I guessed this was her main pleasure

45

in life, just wandering up and down her private road, sneering at intruders while pretending her dog needed a shit. I smiled at her as if I was George Michael's latest toy boy. She glared back.

The houses were vast and ostentatious, but there was something childish about their design, as if what their owners' millions had afforded them was the chance to indulge impulses that most of us only ever play out in Lego. My client's home was a Georgian mansion renovated to within an inch of its life. A sweeping driveway led to an elevated front door flanked by Doric columns, an entrance so grand that it risked overhyping what was inside.

The door was answered by an extremely handsome blond man in a suit, his trousers so tight that both his testicles were on proud display. I almost gasped as I realised I was in the presence of a *butler*. He felt like a unicorn, something you expected to encounter in stories but never real life.

'Matthew,' he said, 'I'm Gustav. Let me take you to Beatriz.'

Gustav led me across an echoing marble floor to the kitchen. The room was dominated by a central island almost as large as my local Pret, filled with plates of salads that didn't skimp on the pomegranate and would have made for an impressive spread at a wedding. Helping themselves were two small boys accompanied by a nanny, while Beatriz — presumably — hovered nearby. She was beautiful and very thin, dressed in loose, feather-light fabrics as if her frame was too delicate to support anything else.

'Eat!' she screamed at one of the boys. 'EAT!'

She looked up as she saw me enter and immediately formed a smile.

'It would be great if you could expand his palate,' said Beatriz without missing a beat. 'He only likes it if it's dry and crunchy.'

I briefly wondered if this was all a big mistake and there was some dietician or child psychologist called Matthew out by the security barrier, trying to gain access while the woman with the spaniel gave him the stink eye. But no, Beatriz appeared to regard it as my job to convince her son to eat something wet and sloppy.

'Felix,' said Beatriz. 'Say hello to your tutor.'

The older boy looked at me. He was short and skinny for his age, with an air of studied nonchalance. He held my gaze, then ignored his mother's instruction and grabbed a handful of nuts.

'Help yourself,' said Beatriz, laughing nervously. 'We don't eat in this family, we graze.'

We what? Presumably she didn't want me to dip my head into the salad bowls and chew from them like a goat. Was grazing some advanced form of eating for people who thought that three meals a day was frightfully bourgeois, or had Beatriz made it up to cover for the fact that she couldn't get her son to eat at the table? Too nervous to graze in front of her, I told her I'd already eaten. In any case, her prominent clavicle suggested she was more interested in food as a tableau than dietary sustenance.

47

'Off you go then,' said Beatriz. 'NO! You can study here.'

She signalled for the nanny and the younger boy to leave with her.

'Can I have a tutor?' said the younger boy.

'No, Theo, you don't need one.'

Theo looked at me proudly.

'I know how penguins shave.'

Satisfied that such a level of knowledge did not require intervention, Theo departed with his nanny and Beatriz.

'Right, Felix,' I said. 'What homework have you got?'

I was inclined to crack some jokes, but the job description had requested a study buddy with a firm hand, and it felt important to establish discipline. Felix showed me his homework sheet.

'Excellent,' I said. 'Describe your dream school trip.'

'Hogwarts.'

'I think it's meant to be somewhere real.'

'The moon.'

I held Felix's gaze. It was impossible to tell if he was being dumb or deliberately perverse, but I strongly suspected the latter. Time to apply that firm hand.

'Maybe it's best if you read the question yourself.'

Felix looked at me as if I had dared suggest he do his own laundry. He picked up his workbook and threw it across the room.

This was a test, wasn't it? I was probably the fifth tutor Felix had pulled this trick on, and if I didn't put a lid on this behaviour Philippa would be advertising for a sixth by the end of the day.

'Don't do that,' I muttered.

I got up to retrieve the book — with an extremely firm hand, it must be said. I had no idea how I was going to unlock my inner disciplinarian, but as I passed the food island, a different thought occurred. We might be screwed when it came to homework, but I could at least have a crack at the secondary brief.

'Here,' I said, crossing back over to Felix. 'I got you some hummus.'

Me: Hey Joel! Not sure if you got my last message. Let me know if you're around :)

FLAT LISTING:
Self-contained studio flat,
BARGAIN PRICE! £70 a week
Zone 1, incredible location
Contact Bib on 07891 197475

Me: That price is insane for Zone 1
Zoe: Contact Bib!!!

Sunday, 25 January, Elephant and Castle

My new year's resolution was to get to grips with my writing ambitions. Relations with the couple in Holloway Road were increasingly strained following one too many encrusted bowls of bean soup left on the side and a chillingly polite note about which way to put knives in the dishwasher. I was finding it harder and harder to be amused by their T-shirts, and had decided to leave before I was found dead with the words May Contain Prosecco gouged in my chest. To be a serious writer, I needed solitude in which to craft my magnum opus. An initial browse of Gumtree suggested that my options were moving to Solihull or finding a sugar daddy willing to finance the cost of a serviced apartment. Then I came across an advert that sounded too good to be true.

The sensible course of action would have been to trust my first instinct. Instead I arranged an appointment with Bib. She lived in the basement flat of a terrace whose white exterior had long been turned grey by road fumes. She answered the door in a papoose containing what I presumed was a baby, though she had such a mad look in her eye that I wouldn't have been surprised if it was a ferret or some fruit she was attempting to ripen. She wore thick black eyeliner and auburn curls piled high on her head in a style that wasn't so much messy bun as psychotic meringue.

'Nice to meet you,' she said. 'I'm Bib.'

The promise of Bib's Gumtree ad fell apart almost immediately. The self-contained studio flat was only a self-contained studio flat in the sense that a studio flat is effectively a room. This one wasn't even self-contained, since the bathroom was across the corridor.

'But,' said Bib, 'it is your personal *private* bathroom.'

I had been hoping for some chic loft space, certainly not the sort of place where I had to be assured of the privacy of my own bathroom in such an ominous tone. But the reason for the bargain price was that the self-contained studio flat was attached to a self-contained family home. As Bib showed me along the corridor, a soldier ran out and fired a machine gun at me. In a show of good humour, I mimicked the impact of the bullets pelleting my skull. The soldier was delighted, and ran away chuckling. Moments later, he returned accompanied by a witch. As the spiritual heir to Maria von Trapp, I didn't need asking twice to improvise on the spot with a four-year-old witch. But I had no desire to get into some kind of *Sound of Music* situation if I wasn't being paid.

'How many children do you have?' I asked Bib.

'Just the five,' Bib said. She patted her papoose, suggesting but still not confirming that it held one of them.

It was hardly an obvious place for a twenty-three-year-old to live. But I had seen blue plaques for famous writers in the most unlikely of locations. With rent this low, I could afford to spend more time writing and less time worrying about bills. I agreed to move in that weekend.

Mum: How was the room?
Me: Cheap and weird
Dad: Sounds very you

NEW JOB ALERT

Job number: 3621

Subject: GCSE English

What: Horace, 16, has been demoted to the intermediate set against his mother's wishes. She is concerned about his new English teacher and wants some support to ensure Horace gains a top grade in his coursework on *Twelfth Night*.

Where: Kensington

When: Wednesdays after school

Wednesday, 28 January, Kensington

Once you were assigned a job, you were provided with the client's full name and address. I had developed a habit of googling not only postcodes but the clients themselves. It rarely turned up more than a LinkedIn profile or some Getty Images from a fundraiser for endangered bears, but when I looked up Carolyn, I discovered that she was the author of a personal blog where she described herself as a 'self-professed yummy mummy'. This was a fascinating way to identify. Was it only here, on her blog, that she professed to yummy mummy status, or did she go around telling people? Maybe Carolyn's word was not to be trusted. An anonymous reader had taken issue with the fact that she claimed to be a lifelong Kensington resident. 'I'm sorry,' they had written, 'but that's a bit misleading. Didn't she move to *North* Kensington?'

What was wrong with North Kensington? This reader was making it sound like Carolyn had glossed over her investments in North Korea. When I arrived at her address, it was a smart four-storey townhouse that had to be worth several million. Carolyn was very trim and dressed in Ugg boots and a fur gilet. In fact, it's what I would have worn if I was going as a yummy mummy to a fancy dress party.

'It's all a bit of a mystery, Matt,' Carolyn said as if we were old friends. 'Historically Horace was *always* in the top third of his year.'

I presumed she meant the lower end of the top third, since here was a woman who would not have hesitated to place her son in the top quarter or fifth, nor even to whip out a pie chart highlighting his flair for algebra, had the data allowed. This job was beyond the usual remit of a study buddy, but I had written my own GCSE coursework on the play in question and had convinced Philippa to let me branch out.

'Horace is waiting for you in his room,' said Carolyn.

She made it sound like she was operating a brothel, but apparently it was only me who found it weird that I was regularly sent to teach in my pupils' bedrooms. I made my way up to the top floor, passing a room with an exercise bike that I imagined Carolyn punishing herself on each morning. Horace was chubby and chirpy, with a weird familiarity which made me wonder if he had got me confused with another tutor. But no — it was that upper class confidence again. Beyond that, Horace didn't present much evidence of his heady days in the lower end of the top third. He was keen to get this over with, but appeared to think it was something that would happen without any input from him.

'What did you think of the text?' I asked.

'I haven't read it,' Horace said cheerily. 'But I've seen the film.'

'Oh, OK. What did you think of that?'

Horace stared at me as if this question couldn't possibly have been anticipated.

'To be honest, I wasn't really watching.'

I quickly learned that this was Horace's modus operandi — offering some bold but foolish response, then capitulating the moment it was questioned. As he began to write an essay plan, Horace was brimming with self-belief. Then I asked if he wanted to include some quotes.

'It's fine,' he said. 'My style is more utopian.'

'Utopian? What do you mean?'

Horace looked flabbergasted.

'I'm not sure.'

I couldn't help wonder if Horace's concerning new teacher was simply the first person in his life to call out his bullshit. It wasn't that Horace was arrogant. He was breezily comfortable with his own limitations, and didn't regard them as any impediment to his progress through life.

'Sir Toby is a parable of gluttons,' declared Horace.

'Do you mean like . . . a caricature of greed?'

'That's it,' Horace said, typing it out exactly.

'Maybe don't — it's meant to be your work.'

Horace looked stunned. Sure, it was *meant* to be his work, but if not this, what was a tutor for? Apparently it was me who didn't get it. As someone who had worked diligently at school, propelled in equal parts by fear and a desperate desire to please my parents, I found it impossible to relate to this level of complacency. Where was the gnawing dread, the consuming competitiveness, the hunger for praise? Horace had the air of someone waiting calmly for a bus, knowing that if he missed it, Mummy could just pop along and give him a lift in the Range Rover. For the rest of the lesson we muddled on in a similar vein. Horace would state something ridiculous about a play he hadn't read, I'd correct him, he'd try to transcribe my thoughts verbatim and I'd put up faint resistance. By the end of the hour, we were less than halfway through.

'Did you get it done?' asked Carolyn when I went downstairs.

'Not quite,' I said.

Carolyn gave me a look which left me in no doubt she was a woman who regularly demanded refunds — and got them.

'Next time then.'

Me:	What do you do if your pupil is terrible at essay writing?
Zoe:	Matt. Do I have to explain
Me:	Even if it's coursework? Isn't that cheating?
Zoe:	I call it collaboration

Thursday, 12 February, Highgate

'Long journey?' said Gustav the butler.

My standard position when tutoring was a desperate desire for approval from both clients and staff, but Gustav was far too attractive to act anything other than rude and aloof. I fielded his small talk primly, until I made the mistake of mentioning that I had recently moved to South London.

'Oh, near Vauxhall?'

'No,' I lied. I was struggling not to look at his balls.

'Interesting area, Vauxhall,' Gustav persisted. '*Very* interesting.'

He gave me a look which made me fear he was referring to the club I'd heard about where you could lie in a trough and have men piss on you. I started waffling about a community café in the Kennington direction. Gustav smiled.

'We should go for a drink some time.'

'Mmm.'

The non-committal mmm was a favourite response of mine that got frequently mocked by my friends, but I found it helped me out of any number of tricky situations. It was a shame I had ruled Gustav out of bounds, since I wasn't exactly spoilt for offers. Joel, the Scottish classroom assistant, hadn't responded to my texts, and I had developed a severe case of writer's block after completing only half of a profile on Guardian Soulmates.

'Is Felix in the kitchen?' I asked quickly.

'No. Cinema.'

'Oh. We did say 4 p.m.?'

'We did.'

Gustav looked offended at the suggestion that his timetabling had been at fault, but I was relieved at the sliver of distance it put between us. As he led me through the garden to a whole other building complex, I realised the mistake had been mine in assuming that being at the cinema precluded Felix from being home — or that the extent of the Northovers' property was contained within four walls. The cinema featured a four-metre-wide screen in front of raked velvet mattresses scattered with bean bags. Felix lay in a heap in the middle, barely watching *Kung Fu Panda* while throwing pieces of popcorn into the air and attempting to catch them in his mouth. He looked up as he saw us enter.

'Please no.'

Gustav smirked and turned to leave.

'I'm not meant to teach you here, am I?'

'Downstairs,' trilled Gustav without looking back.

Of course the cinema had a downstairs. This was like some video game where you kept unlocking new levels. If Gustav ever told me Felix was at the bowling alley, my best bet would be to locate the lift and ask what floor. Felix led me down to the playroom. It seemed a foolish place to study based on name alone. A tiny desk in the corner was only the third most prominent table after pool and air hockey. Felix had English homework again, but this time it was creative writing.

'Great,' I said. 'Any ideas?'

'No,' said Felix. 'You?'

I was starting to think there was something fundamentally silly about sending in a tutor to do homework with a child. They struggled to see the point of me if I was only there to supervise. But it felt equally pointless to put words in their mouths.

'Come on Felix, this is easy. You're allowed to write anything.'

Big mistake. Huge. Felix's eyes flashed with a devious glint and he began to scribble. I once had an English teacher who talked rapturously about the magical potential of the opening line of a story. Within a few words, you could take your reader anywhere from the surface of Mars to inside the mind of a toad. I had always found it an inspiring way to think about storytelling. Felix finished his sentence and looked up with a grin.

Matt was in love with his girlfriend in the pig farm and he ate poo and his girlfriend said oink.

Me: What am I meant to put in his report?
Mum: Say he's very imaginative
Dad: Girlfriend sounds lovely. When can we meet
             her?

Monday, 23 February, Elephant and Castle

There was something appropriate about the fact I'd
gone from teaching in the most expensive square on
the Monopoly board to living a stone's throw from Old
Kent Road, its cheapest. Far from feeling like a down-
grade, whenever I stepped out of a client's house and
headed home, I breathed a sigh of relief. Despite this, I
was already wondering if I'd made a mistake in moving
to Bib's. Yes, the T-shirt couple had been plotting my
death, but at least they plotted quietly. I couldn't tell
you the names of any of Bib's children, but I could
identify them by their various noises. As a writer on
the verge of my first masterpiece, I tried to keep myself
strictly between my self-contained studio flat and my
personal private bathroom. In order to rent me their
(let's be honest) master bedroom, Bib and her husband
had squashed two bunk beds into a smaller room, and
now shared the third with their baby. It wasn't clear
what circumstances led the family to occupy such a
centrally located property while still needing to rent out

a room. I found it hard to get a read on Bib, not least her name, though knowing this country I imagined I'd eventually find out it was somehow short for Susan. To be fair to Bib, she seemed like the kind of person who shared her life story with strangers on a daily basis, but only by keeping my distance did I stand any chance of writing. As I sat down at my laptop, I felt a lot further from the fictional town of Piddle Newton than when I had been living in the real-life town of Wimborne Minster. I closed my eyes and tried to transport myself back there. My mind was filled with the sound of Deborah Meaden on *Dragons' Den*.

I found Bib watching TV in the living room.

'I don't suppose you know any good cafés round here?'

'Cafés?' said Bib. 'There's a McDonald's.'

The woman was a genius. If anything was going to inspire me to write, it was a sausage and egg McMuffin accompanied by a medium cappuccino. I settled in at McDonald's and prepared to make a second attempt at my script. But it was important not to lose sight of my ultimate goal. Two minutes later, I was deep into the Wikipedia page of Dame Judi Dench. I had intended to look up Oscar-winning screenplays, but Emma Thompson proved a gateway drug to an actress wormhole. Before long I had discovered a piece of trivia about Kate Winslet that *had* to be shared with the world. I had recently joined a new website called Twitter which felt like the perfect place to spread the news that the only two times actresses have been Oscar-nominated for playing younger and older versions of the same character in the same film, the younger version was played by Kate Winslet. It took a while to get the phrasing right, but what was that if not honing my craft? Once I was satisfied, I released my mini-masterpiece onto my adoring public of thirty-four followers.

Me: I've done a tweet. Will you like it?

Zoe: I don't know what that means

Wednesday, 25 February, North Kensington

I had done my research and discovered that North Kensington wasn't even technically part of the district of Kensington. It might be packed with fancy delis and multi-million-pound mansions, but it also had pockets of deprivation and a history of riots and slum housing. I could see why that might prompt some snobbery, but it was ridiculous to think that Carolyn's life in North Kensington was anything to be embarrassed about. I had become a regular reader of her blog, where she obsessed over the typical pursuits of a yummy mummy — yoga, shopping and, most of all, her children's schooling.

'Let's make sure we have something good by the time you leave,' said Carolyn pointedly when I turned up.

Horace's teacher was expecting a first draft the following day and Carolyn didn't wish to disappoint. I am not going to claim she winked as she said it. But this was a woman who wanted her money's worth.

Upstairs, Horace was as laid-back as ever. I began feeding him prompts, but his typing was ponderous and I could hear the clock ticking. Then Horace saw an opening.

'How do you spell soliloquy?'

He shifted the keyboard towards me. I swear, in that moment I was only planning to type the word in question. But once my hands hit the keys, something took over me. Why would we finish the essay any other way, when here it was, at my fingertips? It flowed out of me like a symphony. If only I'd known that the answer to all those school essays I'd tortured myself over was to leave the hard part to a paid professional. I wish I could say I felt more guilty. I might easily be helping tip Horace's grade above that of someone who had made a more honest effort. But all I could think about was keeping the client happy. I promised myself this was a one-off.

Matt,
Horace's mother is very happy with your work!
Don't suppose you'd be up for a similar job?
  Philippa

NEW JOB ALERT

Job number: 3705
Subject: English A-Level
What: Katy needs help with her English coursework.
ONE LESSON ONLY.
Where: Edgware
When: Any day, after school

Thursday, 5 March, Edgware

Not everyone was impervious to the recession. I knew I was only a few steps away from becoming the star performer in a lucrative criminal enterprise, but Philippa explained that this client wasn't in a position to pay for more than one lesson. It was unusual to be offered a job rather than scrap it out with other applicants, but it wasn't until I was on my way there that I realised why. The client lived in Zone 6, right at the end of the Northern Line. Looking up house prices here didn't have the same appeal.

As the Tube train emerged above ground and rattled out of the city centre, grand old terraces gave way to modest suburban homes. By the time I had caught a bus and arrived at the pebbledash semi where the client lived, it had taken almost two hours and I couldn't help being glad this wasn't a weekly commute.

Katy answered the door in her school uniform, clutching her book. She was seventeen, poised and less nervous than I was. I looked past her, expecting to see a parent. Normally I'd be delighted not to have to handle some pushy mum or dad, but did that mean we were home alone? Katy took a seat at the dining room table. It was only then it hit me that this was my first female pupil. If I sat opposite, it would be awkward and difficult to teach. But it felt too intimate to sit next to her. What would her parents think if they walked in? For the first time, I wished a client knew I was gay. Maybe I could announce it in the manner of a 1970s sitcom and flamboyantly compliment the net curtains.

'I've got a list of points to go over,' Katy said, glancing at the clock.

All my paranoias vanished in an instant. As I started to teach, Katy quickly proved herself three times the student Horace was. But I was a different person too. Helping Horace cheat felt like a game, down to his mother's winking complicity and his relaxed attitude to our crime. Here, the cost of the lesson was palpable, rather than a rounding error in a vast weekly budget. More importantly, the stakes were real. Katy explained that she had failed her mock exam and would miss out on her university place if she didn't improve.

'Have you done this before?' she asked anxiously.

She meant the book we were studying. But the truth was that this was the first time tutoring had felt like teaching. I was hardly the best man for the job. But I was the person who had come out to Edgware for her one and only hour. I put my head down and did the best I could.

Me:	I think I just taught an actual lesson
Zoe:	WTF. Are you OK?
Me:	Yeah. It felt good.
Zoe:	I will notify the Nobel committee

Monday, 9 March, Highgate

For some reason, being reminded there was a world where people tried hard because there were consequences made me newly inspired to help Felix. Someone like Horace would be fine with or without me. He would struggle through school before landing a place at a prestigious university, where he would struggle, before landing a prestigious job and ultimately some sort of high office. In all likelihood, one of my nieces or nephews would end up tutoring his children.

But Felix — he had issues that ran deeper. He might have every advantage compared to someone like Katy, but that didn't mean this was going to be any kind of quick fix. I needed an ally in the household, but I had no intention of cosying up to Gustav, given that I wanted to ask for directions to the tradesman's entrance whenever he so much as looked at me. My best bet was Zoraida, the family's housekeeper. She was in her fifties, her aquiline features lined with exhaustion. She had been completely uninterested when I introduced myself, and was especially uninterested in my efforts to impress her by speaking Spanish. Naturally this made me desperate to win her over. That day when I arrived, Felix was late getting home from school and Zoraida was in the kitchen, clearing away the latest wedding buffet.

'Can you eat some of this?' she asked. 'They won't.'

As I tried to figure out the correct protocol for eating a giant prawn, Zoraida bemoaned the amount that got made when Felix was so fussy and Beatriz barely familiar with solids.

'She never eats,' Zoraida said. 'Only lemon water.'

'I don't know why,' I said, demolishing a prawn. 'It's delicious.'

Zoraida scoffed.

'Those olives? They taste like urine. And those arti-chokes? Forty pounds a jar.'

'Wow,' I said. 'We should be charging more.'

I immediately regretted speaking so openly. Zoraida talked without deference to our paymasters, but I was the new kid on the block. Had I gone too far?

'*Por favor*, Mateo,' she said. 'Charge what you like. They can afford it.'

We were in business. I prayed that Felix had got held up in traffic and began asking Zoraida all the questions I'd been wondering — namely where Felix's father was and how the family made their money. Zoraida explained that Beatriz was married to George, a prominent hedge fund manager. This was all I needed to know, since hedge funds ranked alongside long division as a concept I was constitutionally incapable of understanding. According to Zoraida, George had always been a workaholic, but since the crash had been working overtime.

'Did he lose money?'

'*Por favor*, Mateo,' said Zoraida. 'He made more.'

I decided that my new goal in life was to make comments so sweetly naive that Zoraida would be compelled to respond '*Por favor*, Mateo' in her Colombian lilt. But for now, I needed to get her advice on Felix.

'*Pobrecito*,' she said. 'They never leave him alone.'

I admitted I was struggling to get him to produce anything of worth in our lessons and wondered if there was a deeper reason for his reticence. Did he see writing as a window into thoughts he preferred to keep hidden?

'Maybe,' said Zoraida. 'But that's what he's learned.'

'What?'

'If he doesn't do it, someone else will.'

Horace: Fuck Matt. We are in some serious shit.

Wednesday, 11 March, North Kensington

Horace and I had swapped numbers after our first lesson so he could message me whenever he forgot the difference between a simile and a metaphor. I had wondered about the wisdom of being on texting terms with a pupil. Now I was grateful for the advance warning. Horace's teacher had provided feedback on the first draft of his coursework. She was only reading in an advisory capacity and couldn't comment directly. However, she had made it clear that one area Horace might like to look at was the whole essay, with a particular focus on it not having been written by someone else.

'Great to have you back,' said Carolyn, clearly annoyed I hadn't wrapped this up already. I wondered how long I had before she started trash talking me on her blog.

'Just need to do a few edits,' I said, charging towards the stairs. Carolyn had been upfront about her expectations, but I imagined she still wanted plausible deniability.

Upstairs, Horace was characteristically chilled about an offence which could easily lead to expulsion.

'We need to dumb it down so it's like a high B, low A,' he said.

'What grades do you normally get?'

'More like a C or D.'

It was the perfect moment to take the moral high ground and tell him I wanted no further part in this subterfuge. But as I read his teacher's comments, a horrible part of me was flattered she had been so impressed with my work. It was a shame it had to be diminished, but here was a further chance to demonstrate my brilliance by reconfiguring it in the style of a merely competent student. If anyone could do it, it was me.

Looking back at the essay, I saw where we had gone wrong. I had tried to keep the language basic, but this had had the effect of making my points crystal clear. Pupils who are insecure about their thinking often over-compensate, mimicking a style they think will make them appear wise. They end up sounding grandiose and confused. Whatever I might like to think, it wasn't something that was easily forged.

'You need to do it yourself this time, Horace. Or your teacher will be able to tell.'

'I don't want to make it bad.'

'No no, just a bit more . . . utopian.'

Me:	I think I avoided getting arrested. That was stressful.
Zoe:	Do you want to come round for dinner?
Me:	I can't, I have to write
Zoe:	Trust me – there's someone I want you to meet

Saturday, 21 March, Clapham

Coming from anyone else, a free plate of moussaka was not worth being subjected to an evening in the company of whichever unthreatening homosexual they had dragged up from the civil service fast stream. But I trusted Zoe. It turned out she wanted me to meet Roland, a friend of her housemate who was an aspiring film director and keen to collaborate with a writer. In the end, Roland cancelled dinner but added me on Facebook. He was the kind of camp posh boy who causes Americans to ask 'Is he gay or just European?' Then I saw that he had commented on a photo of himself wearing a fedora in a nightclub with the words 'The Don'. Perhaps I should have taken this as a warning sign, but I was far too excited. Rather than languish on a laptop in McDonald's, my words were going to be immortalised on celluloid. The Don and I began trading ideas. He urged me to dig deep, claiming there was little he couldn't achieve when he put his mind to it.

'The only limit is your imagination,' he insisted.

This was an optimistic interpretation of a budget of precisely zero pounds, but The Don's enthusiasm was infectious. He told me he wanted our film to capture the gentrification of Soho, so I churned out a ten-page neo-noir mystery with shades of Almodóvar. The Don showered it with praise, while advising that he tended to 'go with the flow' when it came to filming. I wasn't worried. What did it matter how he worked when *I* was the writer?

By the weekend of the shoot, I had told everyone I knew that my first screenplay was going into production. I arranged to meet The Don at a Costa Coffee in Clapham, where he strode in wearing tortoiseshell shades and a Peruvian shawl which looked like it was on back to front. I was disappointed he hadn't completed the look with the fedora.

'Mathieu!' said The Don, pointing at me with both hands held like pistols.

I didn't have it in me to do a two pistol salute in the Clapham branch of Costa, but I greeted The Don and told him I had made a few final adjustments to the script.

'Fuck the script!' The Don declared. 'The camera will write our story.'

I wasn't sure what he meant by this, but in the first instance it required us to head to Tooting. It was there that Nessie, a friend of The Don's, had agreed to lend us the vintage 16mm camera which had apparently taken over screenwriting duties. As The Don began fiddling with the camera, Nessie looked like she didn't trust him with it for a second and declared that she would accompany us on the shoot.

Heading into Soho, my fourth location of the morning, I wondered if we could have done with a shooting schedule. Instead we went with the flow. The Don's self-confidence was mesmerising. As he began taking random shots of bin men and rickshaw drivers, it remained unclear what kind of story the camera was hoping to tell, but it appeared to be one involving minimum wage workers who had not granted the appropriate filming clearances. After a while, it occurred to the camera that our film might benefit from a protagonist.

'I want to shoot you,' said The Don, pointing his lens at me as we stood outside a frozen yoghurt shop. I had officially retired as an actor following my disastrous Edinburgh show, but it was marginally preferable to

71

standing around in the cold. I found myself wandering up and down in front of the yoghurt shop while The Don filmed and Nessie purred approvingly.

'I love the *Stranger in Paris* vibe,' said Nessie.

'He's a rent boy,' said The Don.

I realised I knew very little about this Don character, and had a terrifying premonition that the camera was about to write a scene which involved me providing intimate services to a married older gentleman in full method acting. In the event, The Don got bored and decided he would rather shoot Nessie.

'Can you hold this?' said Nessie, handing me the camera bag and stepping into her new role as The Don's muse. As I watched him at work, I realised he had no greater strategy than making it up as he went along. But while his creation was coming together before his eyes, my script had been consigned to the footnotes of cinema history. He was The Don, and I was bag holder for Nessie from Tooting.

Beatriz: Hi Matt :) Can we see you after Felix's lesson tomorrow? George would like to meet you ;-)

Tuesday, 24 March, Highgate

I would love to ask Beatriz what she felt the wink was achieving. She made it sound like George wanted to check me out for a possible threesome. Despite my earlier curiosity, I had no desire to meet him. I wasn't renowned for my ability to bond with straight men, and I doubted my skills would stretch to a man who had recently posed with a set of dumbbells for an in-depth feature in *Men's Health* in which he self-identified as a 'head honcho'. The piece had given the impression he saw his wife and children as a mild inconvenience, preferring to invest his spare time and energy in his 5 a.m. workout routine and gluten-free pescatarian diet.

'George has found us five minutes,' said Beatriz as I was shown into his study. George was toned, carefully chiselled and had pulled on a hoodie over his work clothes so deliberately that it bordered on camp. He gave me an impatient look to let me know that even five minutes was pushing it. To be fair, I had no idea how long you could leave a hedge fund unattended, and was just as keen as he was to keep this brief. George could meet me, decide about the threesome, then get back to his hedge.

'Felix has exams next term,' said George. 'I gather they're quite important.'

I gathered from his turn of phrase that he wanted me to know he was not the one insisting on their importance.

'Oh yes,' Beatriz said. '*Very* important. They contribute towards the teacher's report which is part of what some schools might use to decide whether or not to give Felix a place.'

I couldn't say they sounded *that* important, but this seemed like something I ought to appear knowledgeable about.

'Mmm.'

'So are you free to help him revise over Easter?' asked George.

'Definitely!'

My response was a bit over-eager. I had just about pulled together a weekly timetable I could afford to live off, but had not yet accounted for the fact that my earnings dropped to nothing whenever a school holiday came around. I had made it through Christmas by the seat of my overdraft, but a few trips to Highgate over Easter would do wonders for my bottom line.

'Excellent,' said Beatriz. 'Do you ski?'

Me: I can't believe you never taught me how to ski

Dad: Outrageous

Mum: I taught you how to play Pontoon

ST MORITZ

I felt like I was in a Bond film. Or a car advert from the '90s. When I landed in Zurich, the efficient Swiss man at the car hire booth had offered me an upgrade for no extra charge. I was most likely doing him a favour by taking a vehicle off his hands that was completely impractical for ski season. By the time that thought occurred to me, I was cruising up into the Alps in a white Mercedes convertible. Cruising is a generous term for someone who had taken three attempts to pass their driving test and only truly felt at ease in a dodgem. Beatriz had claimed the car would give me some independence, which I took to mean the family wanted me to give them theirs. As I — how shall I put this? — skidded into St Moritz and pulled up outside the Northovers' chalet, Beatriz emerged in a snood, looking horrified.

'Matt,' she said. 'Is that the car we booked you?'

I immediately realised my error. The car that had been arranged was considered suitable for a member of the household staff. I had upgraded to something hideously inappropriate. I explained what had happened, but Beatriz practically shuddered at the notion of a free upgrade.

'Come inside,' she said with a warmth that felt like pity. 'You're just in time for breakfast.'

She led me up a stairwell where we emerged into a huge open-plan living room with wooden beams you could literally smell. I wondered if timber really retained its scent that vividly or a housekeeper went round spraying it out of a bottle. George and Felix were seated at a long dining table, while Theo sat playing in the corner with his nanny, operating as they did as a sort of satellite unit to the rest of the family. But there was someone else present — a bearded man in his thirties who was overseeing a breakfast edition of the obscene platters I had seen in London. He introduced himself as Curtis with a jaunty Australian accent and asked how my journey had been, his greeting far more friendly than anyone else's. But it was only a prelude to the one thing he really wanted to know.

'How do you like your eggs? Scrambled? Benedict? Hemingway?'

Were those the only options? I had no idea what the rules were when it came to a personal chef. Was it acceptable to ask for a custom dish? What if I only wanted Ready Brek? There was no question I liked my eggs scrambled, though I never trusted anyone to cook them to my liking. Only a real prat would claim to like their eggs Hemingway.

'Hemingway,' I said.

I had no idea what I had ordered, but it sounded like the kind of thing a rich person had for breakfast. I was sure that even if Curtis handed me a plate of eggs drenched in rum, I could finish them off. What felt like moments later, Curtis placed some in front of me featuring nothing more exciting than a bit of salmon.

'How good are Curtis's eggs?' Beatriz asked before my first mouthful was past my tonsils. 'Aren't they the best?'

'Mmm.'

'Curtis once made the most amazing frittata on our yacht in Capri.'

Beatriz began fondly recalling Curtis's previous culinary hits, up to and including a bagel he made George at a conference in Paris. To be honest, the eggs were average, but I suppose when you take a personal chef on holiday it's important to convince yourself the expense has been worth it.

'Apparently Leo's in town,' said Beatriz. 'DiCaprio,' as if this detail hadn't been necessary for anyone to know who she was talking about. 'Apparently' was the other key word here, since there was no evidence the rumour was true, nor any indication where Beatriz had sourced it. As she began rattling off other celebrity sightings of years past, George read the paper and Felix played on his games console.

'I once saw Ed Miliband in a supermarket in Portsmouth,' I offered.

I looked up to see a teenage girl in a ski suit and a pixie cut, worn with the poise of someone who had been the first in her school to go for such a bold hair-style, even though she had actually been the fourth. I had been told about Felix's older sister Esme, but as she was at boarding school I had completely forgotten about her existence. Esme looked at me with only very mild curiosity.

'Is Matt coming skiing?'

'Oh no,' I said hurriedly. 'I don't ski.'

The family reacted as if I had said I don't bother with toilet paper. In fact, I had once got very close to taking a skiing lesson in the Andes during a brief trip to Chile — an unremarkable anecdote which I had workshopped into an endearing high farce to explain my lack of skiing prowess. Now the moment was here, I bottled it.

'What about dinner tonight?' said Esme.

I sensed she was keen on my presence, though I had no idea why.

'Yes! Of course,' said Beatriz, clearly not having thought about it before that moment. George looked up from his paper in irritation.

'Have we sorted out when Felix is going to study?'

Beatriz burst to life elaborating various scenarios, each of which caused Felix to groan. George remained silent, watching as Beatriz exerted herself to arrive at the only possible answer, which was that everything had to revolve around him. George was operating a reduced work schedule, and that meant there was a routine. Lessons would have to take place *after* Felix had been skiing all day.

'Won't he be exhausted?' Esme asked.

But George shrugged. That wouldn't be his problem. It would be mine.

As the family headed out into the cold and I stayed behind by the radiator, I didn't envy them. But my smugness was short-lived. From the window, I could see people zig-zagging down the slopes, moving with a rhythm most of them had perfected as children. When my classmates in school had headed off to ski each winter, I had told myself there was nothing appealing about a cold weather holiday. But then they returned all healthy and tanned and full of tales about that time Pandora nearly fell off the ski lift. Apparently you had to be there.

I hated that this was how they had made me feel. You could know rationally that your life was full of blessings, only for rich people to make you *feel* like it wasn't enough. Why was I so desperate to fit in? In need of some air, I walked into town. Alpine architecture was surprisingly nondescript, from the outside at least, and with the roads uniformly lined with grit and sludge, St Moritz looked less like an enclave for the rich than I had been expecting. But I was beginning to spot the signs. A family traipsed past in their ski wear and I noticed that the adult looking out for the children on the road was not one of the parents, who were blithely chatting up front, but a nanny anxiously bringing up the rear. As the mother passed, she glanced down at my trainers. What was it about shoes?

Now I was nervous about what to wear for dinner. My standard tutoring uniform was chinos and a checked shirt which made me look like a Mormon missionary whose abstinence policy led to him having a wet dream every four to five days. Rich people had a way of dressing casually which only served to highlight their wealth. One of the richest men I'd ever met wore exclusively shorts and carried his own bottle of ketchup around with him. But that was the kind of self-assurance you couldn't buy. I was going to need more than shorts and ketchup. The central shopping street was filled with designer names — the kind of shops I'd never dream of entering ordinarily. But as I browsed the window displays, I saw a pair of Dior trainers. These weren't the shoes of an unqualified peripatetic teacher who couldn't ski. They were the shoes of a rich man, and I needed them to be mine.

The shop contained no customers and five sales assistants. They wore uniform black, but each had some striking haircut or body modification to let you know they were individuals underneath. It was an absurd number of staff, but maybe there was a time of day when people flooded the place, requiring individual attention. Certainly the staff's heavy presence hadn't been designed for this moment, as they seemed surprised, if not outright annoyed, to see me enter.

'Could I try on that trainer in the window?' I asked nervously.

'He means the sneaker,' said the assistant with blue hair.

The assistant with a nose ring asked my size and sloped off to a back room, so smoothly that I suspected it wasn't a question of volunteering but a strict unspoken hierarchy that was of utmost importance to the self-worth of the four higher-ranking assistants. As I waited, I felt them judge me. The assistant returned with my shoes. The moment I put them on, the mood of the room transformed. All five assistants cooed their approval. The chorus was impeccably rehearsed and not connected to the view before them. There was no doubt they would have executed it just as well had some ungainly woman in a fur coat been tugging on a pair of lime green kitten heels. But it worked. I couldn't help thinking of that Mastercard advert. The cost might plunge me deep into my overdraft, but easing my sense of inadequacy? That was priceless. The assistant with vintage glasses took me to the back of the shop to complete the transaction, while the assistant with a wrist tattoo put the shoes in a bag. Maybe they did only get one customer at a time, and this phalanx of attendants was part of the effect. If so, my private performance had come to an end. The assistant with a shaved head opened the door for me and I stepped outside into a bracing blast of cold air. It was a shame they hadn't asked if I'd like to walk out wearing my new purchase, since all I wanted to do was send a photo to Zoe. But that's probably the last thing a rich person would do. Besides, picture messages from abroad were expensive.

It is hard to imagine a worse time to teach than after skiing. Even without having ever done it myself, I could tell that Felix got in from the slopes feeling shattered, as a day's worth of adrenaline highs came crashing down simultaneously. It didn't help that I was forced to wait around all day doing nothing, like a tennis player whose match has been scheduled last at Wimbledon. Felix, on the other hand, had been at it in the men's doubles and was furious he had to play another round.

'My dad wouldn't let me do the black run,' he declared as he strode in, kicking off his snow boots. 'Asshole.'

The swearing was new, but I barely bothered to caution him. Felix tore open a packet of crisps and ate one with a scowl, then threw the packet over his shoulder. The crisps spilled all over the carpet.

'What did you do that for?'

'Cheese and onion. Gross.'

'Who do you think is going to clear it up?'

'The cleaner,' Felix replied, looking at me as though I was an imbecile.

Something inside me snapped.

'God, you are so *spoilt.*'

We stared at each other. Neither of us could quite believe what had slipped out.

'No I'm not,' Felix said, wounded.

I got up and put the crisps back in the packet. It was ridiculous of me to speak to a child like that, but my irritation was heightened due to a discovery moments earlier. I was looking for some blank paper when I came across a note written by the people who cleaned the chalet for the Northovers. 'We've been working for you for ten years,' they had stated, 'and we've never received a tip.' The thought of them having to clear up Felix's crisps had tipped me over the edge, and a part of me was secretly pleased. What if it was this which made Felix a worthwhile project? I struggled to get excited about his exam results, but I was up for the challenge of changing his attitude.

That night, we drove to the top of the mountain. In a spectacular coda to my shopping trip, I had decided I was too self-conscious to wear my new shoes. Beatriz told me several times that Gustav had booked us the table with the best view, which I'm sure it was during daylight. At night the panorama was dark and foreboding. The restaurant was an unassuming alpine tavern like every other building in town. But when I opened the menu, words like foie gras and gold leaf leaped off the page.

'Have whatever you want,' George insisted.

The last time someone had made me this offer, my brother and I were at a Beefeater with our grandparents, and had obliged by ordering the astonishingly named Horn of Plenty. I couldn't bring myself to go for a risotto that somehow cost €60, but it was obvious the Northovers wanted to treat me. I opted for frogs' legs.

'How fun!' Beatriz grimaced.

As Beatriz ordered a salad and George an off-menu omelette, I realised I had got it wrong again. The menu might have encouraged gourmet eating, but the Northovers intended to show me it was beneath them. What was the point of coming somewhere like this if you weren't going to splash out? Thank god I hadn't worn the sneakers. Travelling with a client was a minefield compared to going to their house for an hour once a week. Luckily I wasn't the only one falling foul of their standards. The table next to us ordered a £5,000 bottle of Dom Perignon, and finally the family had something to bond over.

'So problematic,' Esme said.

'It's not problematic,' said George. 'It's tacky.'

Esme shrugged. 'It's just really capitalist.'

She beamed at me as if she was speaking at the vanguard of economic theory. It's not like I didn't broadly agree with her, but you don't want to give too much encouragement to people of limited ideas and copious means. It wouldn't take much for Esme to spend the next three years at art school conceiving a performance piece called 'Capitalism Mais Pourquoi?' which would consist of her burning items from her own designer wardrobe and would receive coverage in the *Evening Standard* after having its opening night attended by Lady Victoria Hervey. I said as much as it took to placate Esme without compromising any of my wider political principles. Then a waiter arrived with my frogs' legs.

I had woken at 3 a.m. to catch my flight, and had been ready for bed for hours. But the day held one more surprise. Outside the restaurant, Curtis was waiting for us. I'd presumed he had been given the night off, but there he was, standing with a pile of sledges and not quite hiding his look of resentment.

'It's a tradition!' said Beatriz.

'Lame,' said Esme.

Felix glanced up at me, making sure he was out of his sister's earshot.

'It's actually kind of cool.'

We each took a sledge and set off down the mountain. When I arrived at the bottom, Curtis was waiting for us with the Jeep. He loaded up the sledges and drove us back up to do it all over again. I had grown up near a country park and remembered snowy days when we'd take our sledges to whizz down the hill, then trudge up with hot red cheeks and repeat the cycle until we were exhausted. I wish I could say it was more satisfying that way — that the trudging made the whizzing more of a rush. But as Curtis whisked us up in the Jeep, I caught myself wondering how I'd ever stood the alternative.

Me:	I can't believe you used to make me carry my own sledge up the hill
Mum:	Are you drunk?
Dad:	Better report us to social services

From then on, we settled into a routine. I didn't have to tutor until 3 p.m. each day, meaning that before then I could work on my script. Virginia Woolf wrote that a woman needs money *and* a room of her own in order to write. Turns out if you are a man with a luxury ski chalet and a personal chef at your disposal, you become very productive. I was on a roll with my heartwarming comedy set in the fictional town of Piddle Newton, and had introduced a hilarious subplot involving a pop star disguised as Winnie the Pooh. In the gap between writing and lessons, I visited the sun deck to use the jacuzzi and imagine my forthcoming appearance on *Graham Norton*. One day, as I tipped my head back, I caught one of the staff in the next door chalet looking at me. They immediately got back on with their cleaning, but I blushed hard. I wanted to call out and let them know I was an employee taking a break, not one of those awful rich people we both work for. Instead I closed my eyes and let the bubbles tickle me.

Following our clash over the crisps, Felix's disdain for lessons was reduced to a sulky reluctance. This didn't make them any more productive.

'What do you call it when water turns to gas?'

'H_2O.'

'No, that's the chemical formula for—'

'Water.'

'Yes, but—'

'Condensation.'

'No, listen to the question.'

'Is it cumulonimbus?'

Our issues extended beyond the curious British obsession with teaching young children professional meteorological terminology. Felix's mind was full of information

— the correct information, no less. But he had no ability to process it logically. It was a habit I had noticed in him, where the pressure to answer is so great that you fire out a piece of knowledge, *any* knowledge, rather than grapple with doubt, possibility and reason even for a moment. I told Felix the most useful thing he could learn was to pause for five seconds before answering any question. He paused for five seconds to consider what I had said.

'That is *such* a waste of time.'

'Come on, Felix. These exams are really important.'

'Says who?'

'Your mum.'

Felix burst out laughing, and I realised how rare it was to see his face light up. But jokes aside, Beatriz was on our case. She became increasingly keen for progress updates, approaching me at mealtimes and asking 'How's our little soldier?' I wasn't wild about characterising Felix as a dinky member of the military industrial complex, but I ran with her metaphor and said something about him being a trooper. This didn't satisfy her, and she began making unscheduled visits to our lessons. She had observed that I was too polite — the word I am looking for is cowardly, but let's go with polite — to ever decline the offer of a coffee. Apparently there was no variety Curtis couldn't whip up, but I wasn't sure if he could actually be bothered or was praying for me to stick with an Americano. 'Would you like a macchiato?' Beatriz asked one day. 'Curtis does a wonderful version.' Another time, I agreed to a frappé so large I had to pour half of it down the toilet. Then one day, George got home from his black run earlier than planned and caught her red-handed.

'Leave them alone,' he hissed.

'I'm *taking* Matt a latte.'

'Get Curtis to take it up, for god's sake.'

It was as if seeing his wife complete a domestic task was an insult to the lifestyle his earnings afforded. But Beatriz had no intention of ceasing operations. She did what any self-respecting supplier would and went underground. I looked up one day to see her standing there holding a flat white. She had made it up the stairs without making a sound or spilling a drop, by what method I know not. The next day, she waited until George had gone out, then materialised with a hazelnut cappuccino. A short while later, she came racing back into the room.

'He's coming! Hide it!'

I couldn't believe she was serious, but Beatriz wouldn't leave until I'd hidden the cappuccino under the desk. She made it back downstairs moments before George walked through the door.

Her behaviour was fast becoming deranged. But Beatriz had lost sight of her original goal of keeping tabs on our lessons. George's prohibition provoked a desire to rebel. For a few sweet days, my personal drinks service continued. By our last morning in St Moritz, Beatriz had got complacent. As she lingered to chat shortly after depositing a cortado, a figure appeared behind her.

'What are you *doing* in here?' George fumed. 'I *told* you to stay out.'

He looked at Beatriz with a rage that hardly felt commensurate to the offending cortado. Her response, astonishingly, was to tiptoe backwards out of the room like some mad *Looney Tunes* character. Standing on the landing, observing the scene, was Esme.

'Why do you let him treat you like that?' Esme said to her mother. 'I can't stand it.'

It was the most I'd liked Esme all week.

'Don't listen to her,' George said to Beatriz.

'See!' said Esme. 'This isn't normal!'

Even George was flummoxed. I ought to have been embarrassed, but my thoughts were with Felix, who was observing the scene with a trembling lip. There are few things more heartbreaking than a child who is trying very hard not to cry. As a tutor I had been let so casually into the heart of my clients' lives, but this was the first time I had the sense that I was seeing behind the curtain. Whatever this family's dysfunction, it went beyond a couple of coffees.

The next day, the weather was beautiful. We were due to travel home, but George declared the skiing too good to miss. I suspect no one could bear the idea of leaving on the heels of such a fallout. Felix's lessons were cancelled, and Beatriz insisted I had a go at skiing. This had been mooted at various points throughout the week, always with an air of courtesy. Now it felt like a command.

We headed en masse to the nursery slope, where my fellow debutants were largely prepubescent and included

89

several toddlers. We watched, I swear to god, an actual baby execute a perfect run down the slope. Few things in life count for more than a head start. There was no way I wasn't going to embarrass myself.

Felix took charge of instructing me, telling me how to bend my legs and balance my weight.

'It's pretty simple,' he insisted.

It was sweet to see him in this role. Maybe he had enough authority figures in his life, and I needed to lean more into the buddy side of my job description. The task for now was making it down the slope without decapitating the heir to the Rothschild fortune. There was no immediate risk of this, as I fell over on my first six attempts.

'You're so bad at this,' said Felix, laughing as I tumbled yet again.

'Yep,' I said, grinning. 'I'm the worst.'

I realised I was playing my part to perfection. Everyone was enjoying the spectacle, with even George cracking a smile as I accidentally did the splits and yelped in pain. I wasn't sure where spraining my joints for the amusement of a wealthy patron fell in Esme's capitalist analysis, but it was a job no one else could have taken on. Only I was free to glide above the Northovers' intra-family warfare — if by glide I meant the kamikaze runs I was making down the slope. I was happy to give the family something to laugh about, but it was seeing the change in Felix that really pleased me. I'd assumed he would get bored and rush off to terrorise some black runs. But for hours he stayed on the slope, making a huge effort to explain things in terms I'd understand as I fell face first into the snow.

The next morning, we took a car to the airport. I had heard George calling Gustav to rebook our flights and asking him to 'see if they have any PJs'. It was an odd request, but maybe pyjamas were part of the service when you flew first class. As we arrived at what amounted to a hangar and a field, I realised George had been after a little more than a pair of pyjamas — he had booked a private jet.

Nothing about the check-in process convinced me that private airfields aren't the backbone of global crime networks. This is not to suggest there was anything untoward about our flight, only that I imagined an international crime lord could very easily pass through here, and presumably had done many times. Our pilot greeted us with such a precise combination of sycophancy and good cheer that I guessed he had only recently been awarded a large tip for ferrying a group of strippers to a bunga bunga party. A woman purporting to be a customs officer gave so cursory a glance at my passport that I was sure if it had been an old building society pass book she would have waved it through.

The pilot's second-in-command was doubling as the flight steward, and did a half-hearted safety demonstration before pointing at some sandwiches to which we could help ourselves during the flight. George looked embarrassed. Presumably one can have a full staff and champagne on tap for the right price, but this was the PJ that was available at short notice. He had gone to the trouble of hiring a private jet and ended up with identical catering to a parish council meeting.

'Dad, I hope you carbon offset this,' said Esme.

'You can get the coach home if you prefer,' said George.

Since camping holidays had involved catching the ferry to Calais with our trailer tent, I had not been on a plane between starting school and turning seventeen. When I finally did, it was a school trip and my class-mates couldn't believe the juvenile thrill I got from taking off. In the years since, I had learned to control my excitement. But speeding down the runway, it took everything I had not to squeal.

On the ground, the lack of other passengers had been a convenience, but up in the air it was something more. Cruising through the sky in our own little bubble with views on both sides, there was an unmistakable feeling that the flight was for *us*. I knew that wealth bred a sense of exceptionalism, but this was the first time I had experienced the sensation. It was impossible to convince yourself it was rationally necessary — the next logical step was starting to believe you were a little bit special, that you deserved it somehow. I would like to say I was observing all this with detachment. The truth is I had never felt more swept up.

Before I had time to convince myself of my own supe-riority, we were landing in England. We stepped onto the tarmac and straight into two chauffeured cars which whisked us twenty metres or so to a waiting helicopter.

'Eight of you, is it?' the helicopter pilot asked.

'Seven,' said George.

I shuffled to the front.

'How are you getting out of here then?'

I gave the pilot a sheepish look.

'Taxi to Elephant and Castle.'

The family took off in the helicopter and I was shown into an empty waiting room. After a few moments, a staff member came in looking worried.

'I'm so sorry, sir, but all our Mercedes are booked. Would you mind taking a normal car?'

SUMMER TERM 2009

Zoe:	When can I get a full impression of you skiing?
Me:	Lunch tomorrow? Can't do tonight . . . I'm going on a date :)

Saturday, 18 April, Soho

I was relieved to find my week with the Northovers hadn't made me allergic to public transport. Hopping on to the Tube in my dirty Converse had never felt better. In spite of my impulsive shoe purchase, my fee from the trip meant I had more money in my account than at any time since student loan pay day. I had almost ended up agreeing to a drink with a man who worked for an environmental charity, but that didn't seem wise so soon after stepping off a private jet. Recalling how even Joel the classroom assistant had made me feel guilty, I went for someone who looked like they wouldn't judge me for my recent excesses. Ismael was a marketing manager from Willesden Junction whose photos included one of him drinking pink champagne at a spa hotel. On my own profile, I had taken a significant step. In the box where you put your occupation, I had written 'tutor/writer'. This was a bold move, but I felt more like a writer than ever. The comforts of the Northovers' chalet and Curtis's eggs had allowed me to complete a full draft of my heartwarming comedy set in the fictional town of Piddle Newton. I had read some advice about putting it in a drawer for two weeks then coming back to it, but since I didn't have a drawer to hand I had seen no alternative but to send it out immediately to a random selection of film industry professionals. The only reply I had received so far was a bounce back from Mailer Daemon. But I was sure the bidding war would kick off any minute.

Ismael was waiting for me outside the bar where we had agreed to meet. He looked as attractive as in his photos, but had taken the incredible decision to style his hair into a physics-defying backwards fringe which made him resemble a great crested grebe.

'Stunning!' he said as I walked up.

I was flattered, at least until we entered the venue and it became clear that stunning was Ismael's preferred term for anything remotely positive. The bar was stunning, as was the fact that it had an available window seat. When our piña coladas arrived . . . you get the idea.

'So you're a writer?' said Ismael.

'No,' I said. 'Well . . . no.'

I started mumbling about the script I'd sent out, sounding so apologetic I may as well have told him about one of my recent tweets. I changed the subject to my trip to St Moritz. We were back in reliably stunning territory, with not only the private jet and the frogs' legs but my disastrous skiing attempt passing Ismael's bar. The more he agreed with me, the more I resented him. It was my fault for agreeing to the date. I imagined the conversation I might have had with the charity worker, thoughtfully critiquing my experience with the Northovers and my reasons for finding it so seductive.

'So what actually *is* a study buddy?' asked Ismael. 'Are you like a teacher?'

'Yes. Well, no. Not really. That's why I'm there officially. But it's not what they pay me for.'

Ismael pulled a face.

'I mean it is, but I'm more like . . . a cross between a teacher and a friend.'

It sounded like a perfectly stunning combination, but Ismael looked even more confused than before.

'How does *that* work?'

Dear Matt,
Thank you for sending us your script. It started strongly, but you didn't seem to know where you were going.
    All best,
    Jenny Cuthbert,
    Countdown Films

Tuesday, 5 May, Highgate

As I entered the playroom, I was hit by the scent of Armani Pour Homme. Felix was playing air hockey with a blandly handsome, broad-shouldered man about my age. He was wearing a Harvard University sweater — an item that is only acceptable if intended as a tribute to Princess Di — and narrating their game with wholesome affirmations that made him sound like the clean-cut sports coach in a Nickelodeon series that didn't air in a late enough time slot to give his character any hidden depths. Who was this twit?

'I'm Justin,' said Justin with a smile. 'Felix's Big Buddy.'

Felix's what? If I didn't dislike him already, Big Buddy stepped forward and shook my hand so firmly I nearly yelped. I have always been baffled by the culture of the firm male handshake. There's something preposterous about greeting someone by squeezing one hand extremely hard. I forget it's what men do, and then it's too late and my hand has wilted in their grasp. I can only hope that by then they have got whatever they need from the exchange.

'*Great* to meet you,' said Big Buddy.

He turned to Felix and performed one of those pre-rehearsed routines that starts as a high five and ends with a fist bump and a finger wiggle. I couldn't even handle a standard handshake and these two were already on some advanced bro level. I led Felix over to his desk. This was our final revision session before his exams, but he was a fool if he thought my sole interest wasn't getting the lowdown on Big Buddy.

'So what kind of thing do you two do together?'

'Fun stuff,' said Felix. 'We did Laser Quest this week.'

Was there *anything* this family didn't outsource?

'That's cool,' I said. 'Who won?'

If it had been Felix, I would judge Big Buddy for his shameless pandering. If Big Buddy had won, it was his ego I would condemn.

'We teamed up,' said Felix, 'and beat some Japanese tourists.'

There it was — indisputable proof that Big Buddy was a racist.

'Do you remember how bad I was at skiing?'

'Yeah,' Felix chuckled. 'I was telling Justin.'

Of *course* he and Big Buddy had mocked me behind my back. There was only room for one buddy in this town. I had to defeat him.

NEW JOB ALERT

Job number: 4124

Subject: Homework help

What: Twins! Two American boys need someone fun and lively to help them after school. £5 supplement on top of your regular hourly rate.

Where: Kensington Palace Gardens

When: Mondays and Thursdays, 5 p.m.

Me: Check out the address

Zoe: Nice. You're basically teaching Prince
William.

Thursday, 14 May, Kensington

I had hit the jackpot. Kensington Palace Gardens is regularly cited as the most expensive street in the country, if not the world. A steel magnate had allegedly bought a house there for £70 million. As I passed the eponymous palace at the top of the road, I quite liked the idea of becoming a regular visitor. Maybe I'd bump into Prince William eventually, or at least catch his eye from a bathroom window as he did a wee. The wedding cake mansions that followed Kensington Palace were no less palatial. But as I reached the modern block of flats where I was heading, I found that its entrance was not technically on Kensington Palace Gardens, but a different street more easily accessed without ever crossing the famous one next door. Apparently it wasn't only in North Kensington that people fudged the truth about their address.

The building had all the character of a hotel that mainly hosts conferences. Aside from a concierge, it was eerily quiet, with one of those ultra-efficient lifts which meant I was still checking my hair in the mirror when the lift opened and I found myself right at the client's door. Waiting for me was the twins' mother, Belinda.

'Ignore this,' she said, gesturing at lips that were swelled with filler. 'Allergic reaction.'

Belinda was wearing a velour tracksuit and was trailed by a panting Chihuahua. As she showed me in, she reeled off a list of her allergies. The apartment was cream and impersonal, though that only highlighted the spectacular view of the park. I noticed a chair wrapped in plastic, unsure if it was newly delivered or this was some sort of look.

'The twins are doing so well at school,' Belinda said.

She began flicking through their exercise books and announcing their past test scores like some hyped-up judge on *Strictly Come Dancing*. 'Ten! Ten! Nine! And another ten!'

It was a relief to hear someone show confidence in their children. But if they were doing this well, why did they need a tutor? Before I could ask, Belinda's phone began to ring and she pointed me down the hall to where the twins could be found. In their room, two eleven-year-old boys with identical cow's lick fringes were playing a computer game.

'Ooh, is that Grand Theft Auto?'

'No,' they said with simultaneous disdain.

My one chance to impress them and I had blown it. I had been proud of myself for referencing something more contemporary than Simon the Sorcerer.

'You must be Harry and Hayden.'

They shared a look and told me which was which. Harry was wearing glasses while Hayden wasn't. It struck me immediately. Harry Potter! That was easy. They showed me their homework and got started on it with minimal fuss. I sat back, keeping an eye on their progress without doubting for a second that I would soon be announcing their latest perfect scores.

'You might want to check that spelling, Harry.'

Harry looked up at me.

'I'm Hayden.'

Wait, what? I thought Harry was the one with the glasses. Hayden Potter didn't have the same ring to it, but apparently that's what we were working with. I corrected myself and let them get back to it. A short while later, Harry excused himself and went to the loo. Hayden kept his head in his book, and my mind wandered to an overpriced coconut doughnut I was going to buy on the way home with my £5 twin bonus. Then I looked up. Standing in the door was Hayden Potter.

I looked back at Hayden, who I had thought was at the desk. But seated there was Harry. Or was it? A frown of confusion spread across my face.

'I'm Hayden,' said Hayden, presumably.

'I'm Harry,' said Harry with a smirk.

Yes I got that, you little shitbag. But how had I got them so mixed up? I regretted not giving them less confusing nicknames, such as Shitbag and Ron Weasley. Then Shitbag grinned at Weasley, and I realised what had happened. *They were trying to confuse me.* Either they had lied, swapped glasses, or each had a pair — my brain was no longer capable of telling. Shitbag and

Weasley fell about laughing. No doubt they had pulled this routine on dozens of people. I had initially been relieved to learn how bright the twins were. Now I was scared they were going to outfox me.

> Dear Matt,
> Thank you for giving us the opportunity to read your script. I'm afraid it's not one for us.
>> Regards,
>> Michael Satchel,
>> Paravel Productions

Sunday, 24 May, Waterloo

I was starting to question my strategy of blowing every conceivable contact on the same rushed draft of my only script. It wasn't the ideal time to attend a festival for young filmmakers, but Zoe said I'd regret not going. Knowing of my recent sacrifice to the House of Dior, she even offered to buy me a cocktail beforehand. We sat on the South Bank of the river, surrounded by young adults enjoying a well-earned break from their busy careers. I had no sense that I was among them. The script rejections were bad enough, but I admitted I was feeling equally lacking as a study buddy. I told Zoe my regret at taking on twins.

'Interesting,' Zoe said. 'More boys.'

103

I hadn't failed to notice this trend of matching tutors and students by gender. Apparently most parents expressed a preference, but Zoe thought it was less a safeguarding concern than a more lofty hope that we would serve as some kind of role model to their child.

'I feel like anyone who hires me as a role model for boys deserves a refund.'

'Bullshit,' said Zoe. 'Take their money. Plus why shouldn't any girls get to have you as their role model?'

'I don't want to be anyone's role model!'

I told her how inadequate I felt in the face of Big Buddy and his brand of athletic masculinity. My parents had never batted an eyelid at my habit of befriending girls and collecting Sylvanian Families, but at school I had quickly realised I was going to struggle without a more convincing vote of support for the breasts of Lara Croft.

'What the fuck even is a Big Buddy?' I said. 'He's like two inches taller than me. Big wow.'

'Matt, he's not *your* Big Buddy. The question is where are Felix's real buddies?'

I felt a rush of sympathy for Felix, and recounted the dramatic events of St Moritz. Big Buddy aside, I was starting to feel responsible for him.

'You've bonded,' Zoe said. 'You're part of the buddy collection.'

'Except I can't get him to study.'

'That isn't your only value to him.'

'Try telling that to his parents. They're obsessed with these stupid exams.'

I hoped Zoe would reassure me that the exams weren't as important as Beatriz had made out, but she confirmed the opposite. Competition for senior school places was fierce and it really could come down to knife-edge criteria like past exam records and school reports.

'Fuck. So I do need to get him working.'

'If you want to keep that job, then yeah.'

It didn't occur to me to pause and consider whether I did want to keep working for a family that was drawing me deeper into their dysfunctional dynamic by the week. Zoe promised it would get easier, and suggested a tactic that had worked well with a tricky pupil of hers — arranging a meeting with their teacher.

We went inside to the festival. The auditorium was packed with aspiring filmmakers like me, but as with the other tutors in the holding pen, I couldn't bear to acknowledge that any of them were real people with legitimate dreams and scripts that might even be — god forbid — better than mine. The event featured a panel attempting to convert their highly specific experiences of breaking into the industry into some suitably generalised platitudes. A television director emphasised how important it was to take risks, claiming that no one was going to take notice of us otherwise. She was speaking to a full auditorium, but it was clearly me she was addressing. Afterwards I raced over and stopped her at the exit.

'I was really inspired by what you said up there,' I said.

'Happy to help,' said the director, turning to leave.

'So . . . can I send you my script?'

Beatriz: Hi Matt – we'd love you to chat to Felix's form teacher! Good idea!!! Miss Lucas is very friendly. I'll put you in touch!!

Thursday, 4 June, Hampstead

I remember being absolutely stunned to discover that my primary school teachers had first names. Now I wonder if they actively cultivated a sense of distance. Miss Lucas had the kind of blank personal appearance that had been carefully calibrated to avoid any comments from pupils. I suspected every moment of Miss Lucas's working day was carefully planned, as she welcomed me into her classroom with a clipped tone that made clear this could have been an email.

'Thank you *so* much for seeing me,' I said.

'She didn't make you do this, did she?'

'Who?'

'Felix's mum. It won't affect what I put in his report.'

'Oh god no, this was all me. She said you'd be the best person to meet. To be honest, I've run out of ideas.'

Miss Lucas betrayed a flicker of sympathy and gestured for me to take a seat.

'I'm not surprised,' she said. 'Felix has worse motivation than anyone I've ever taught.'

I agreed. But what was her solution?

106

Miss Lucas stared at me.

'I thought that was your job.'

Hold on. I had come all the way here on the understanding that Miss Lucas would tell me exactly what to do and how to do it, so I could earn praise from Beatriz and get ahead in the race against Big Buddy. But Miss Lucas was just getting started.

'He doesn't *want* to work,' she said. 'He feels that very deeply. So unless you can crack that nut—'

As she spoke, she crossed to retrieve a stray pencil she had spotted underneath a desk. I glanced at a wall filled with maths charts and diagrams. I bet Miss Lucas could do long division in her sleep. As she mouthed words at me, her eyes narrowed infinitesimally and I realised she knew when someone wasn't listening. If I wasn't careful, she would take away a team point — a disaster I had successfully avoided ever since being busted in Year 2 for scribbling all over the colouring book of my nemesis Matthew Jancey. I snapped back to attention.

'I can think of one solution,' said Miss Lucas. 'But you're not going to like it.'

She checked her watch. Our meeting had taken sixteen minutes, precisely the length she had predicted. If she hurried, she could still make the 17:04 to Muswell Hill, where — there could be no doubt — she had a delicious salmon fillet defrosting in the fridge. I told her I was open to any of her suggestions. Miss Lucas picked up her handbag and gave me her kindest smile.

107

'I can't help wondering if having a tutor makes it worse.'

Zoe:	Wow
Zoe:	I'd like to report a murder

Monday, 8 June, Highgate

Felix couldn't be persuaded to tell me how his exams had gone. It was impossible to know if this meant he had screwed up or he just didn't care. As he waited for his results, his curriculum took on a decidedly end-of-year flavour. One teacher had given up and let his class watch *Mona the Vampire*, but another had set them the elaborate task of building a Saxon village. It was the perfect job for me after years of watching *Blue Peter* as a child. I had entered all their competitions, but my ingenuity was ahead of its time, and I still couldn't believe my spectacular bottlenose dolphin sanctuary had lost the contest to design a new Windsor Safari Park to some dweeb from Bristol who'd had the tedious idea of replacing it with a weather station. Finally, here was a chance for my talents to be appreciated. By Saturday, I had given the village the elegant name of Pendoryn and conceived an innovative method to imitate wattle and daub.

When I walked into the entrance hall, Beatriz was talking to Big Buddy, her face glowing as they spoke.

Why didn't I have that effect on women?

'Matt, have you two—'

'Yes,' I snapped.

'Can Justin help me with my model?' said Felix.

I grimaced as Big Buddy declared he'd be happy to help. Then I realised this was my chance to gain the upper hand. No way could Big Buddy measure up to my model-making prowess. Over in the playroom, I got out my panoply of building materials and outlined my vision. It was important to let Felix feel involved, but the construction of an entire village was not an appropriate job to leave to one so juvenile. I would let Felix exercise his creativity over minor tasks such as the fruit for the village stocks, while taking charge of any wider structural and municipal concerns.

'What about a drawbridge?' said Big Buddy.

A *drawbridge?* The historical inaccuracy was embarrassing. If he had been submitting a competing entry to a *Blue Peter* competition I would have encouraged him to go ahead, but we were in this together and I was going to have to correct him.

'Cool!' said Felix.

As Big Buddy tore into some cardboard I had specifically designated for the weaving house, I held my tongue. It was that one word from Felix that was stopping me. Historical accuracy was perfectly within my brief as a tutor. But it was equally important that Felix prefer me to Big Buddy. I looked at the monstrosity Big Buddy was creating, which would no doubt topple under the weight of the herd of cattle I planned to manufacture from pipe cleaners.

'Awesome,' I said.

Hi Matt,
I read your script! Let me know a good time to call.
  Amanda

Friday, 19 June, Elephant and Castle

'Maybe I'm not the right audience,' said Amanda.

It was hardly an auspicious opening statement. Still, taking a phone call in the glamorous confines of my self-contained studio flat was the closest I had yet got to an industry meeting. Amanda went out of her way to emphasise the positives. There was good news: I could write! The bad news was there was barely anything about the script that she liked.

'The characters said one thing then did the opposite. I couldn't tell if we were supposed to like them or hate them. But my main problem was I didn't know what you were trying to *say*.'

Trying to say? I wasn't trying to say anything. I was trying to win an Oscar. Amanda insisted I had talent, but clearly thought I had bitten off more than I could chew.

'Have you considered writing a short film?'

I had never been so insulted. I couldn't possibly fit all my good ideas and funny lines into a *short*. I would take Amanda's feedback and turn my script into the crowd-pleasing hit with awards potential I knew it was. She suggested that I took a break from it to get some perspective, but didn't they also say to strike while the iron was hot? I resolved to begin the rewrite immediately — or at least, once I had gone to the loo. But when I went to the bathroom, it contained a very tall Frenchman using an electric nose trimmer.

'*Ah, pardon*,' he said, realising he had failed to lock the door.

'*Non, pardonnez-moi*,' I replied.

It was only when I got back to my room that I processed what had happened. Why was there a Frenchman trimming his nose hair in my personal private bathroom? And why had I gaily conversed with him, rather than demanding to know who he was? I went to find Bib, who was watching TV with two to three children draped over her. She looked up as I approached.

'Oh yeah,' she said. 'We've got another lodger.'

'Oh. Is he going to be using my bathroom?'

'No, no, no, no,' Bib said. 'Well, yeah. It would be great if you didn't mention you're lodging here too.'

'He's already seen me! Who should I say I am?'

I don't know what I thought I was doing. There was no doubt this was a woman prepared to hand me a new identity complete with wig and props which she would

111

expect me to fully inhabit for the next six months. But Bib was losing her place in *Come Dine With Me*.

'You'll figure it out.'

Zoe:	I'm telling you – write about Bib! Oscars guaranteed
Zoe:	But sorry the woman didn't like your script

Wednesday, 24 June, Kensington

I remained confused as to why the twins needed a tutor. If they were clever but badly behaved, surely you'd just hire a nanny? Since the task had fallen to me, I was determined they would not defeat me. If Harry or Hayden were challenged academically compared to Harry or Hayden, then perhaps it would be necessary to be able to distinguish between Harry or Hayden and Harry or Hayden. Since this was not the case, there was no need to tell them apart. I resolved to think of them as Twin1 and Twin2.

Today when I arrived, they were wearing their trademark cheeky grins. But shorn of their individual identities, there was nothing they could do to harm me.

'Tell him,' Twin1 said to Twin2.

'Tell me what?'

Twin2 looked at me with a grin.

'We caught you on your phone.'

I had discovered that homework supervision was an excellent time to catch up on my texting. I didn't feel bad, as ever since Miss Lucas's assassination attempt I had decided any pupil capable of doing their homework without me counted as a win. I had a good mind to ask Twin2 what he'd rather I did while he hashed out a six-mark answer to the latest mind-numbing comprehension about a kestrel.

'No, we filmed it,' said Twin1. 'And showed our mum.'

Fuck. I tried to recall what I had been doing on my phone in our previous lesson, but it could have been anything from texting my mum about *You Me Bum Bum Train* (don't ask) to reading a deep dive on the early contenders for next year's Best Supporting Actress Oscar. There was even a slim chance I had been fielding horny solicitations from Ismael who, despite me declining a second date, wouldn't take no for an answer. There was no question some of his messages were grounds to get me fired. At the end of the lesson, my heart was in my mouth. But Belinda was all smiles.

'Thanks Matt!' she said cheerily. 'How did it go?'

'Great,' I said. 'To be honest, they barely need me.'

'No,' said Belinda. 'But everyone else in their class has a tutor.'

I walked out of the building and up Kensington Palace Gardens. It wasn't the fastest route home, but I hadn't lost hope of spotting Prince William. As I looked at the ludicrously large mansions, I understood the difference between here and North Kensington. Out there you might be rich, but you hired a tutor because you needed one. Here it was a status symbol, stealing your children's free time purely so you could look good among the other yummy mummies. Carolyn might like to hide the detail of where she lived. But I couldn't help thinking her kids had the better deal.

Thursday, 25 June, Highgate

'Ay Mateo,' said Zoraida. 'You remind me of my son.'

I looked at the tuna sandwich she was making me from the Northovers' leftovers and held my nose. It was a taste I had despised since childhood, but knowing how much it pained Zoraida to see food go to waste I had told her it sounded delicious. Any resemblance to her son was unlikely to last long, as the more I spoke to Zoraida, the more I exposed the limits of my Spanish. I could tell Zoraida was baffled that such a level had been deemed worthy of a university degree. But she knew the bar was on the floor when it came to British people and foreign languages.

'Have you heard anything about Felix's exam results?' I just about succeeded in asking.

They had been due the previous week, but it had come and gone and no one had said a thing. Felix insisted he hadn't heard and Beatriz was so jumpy I didn't dare ask. I was so keen to know that I had even thawed my strategic frostiness with Gustav to see if he could enlighten me. But Gustav had nothing either.

It had to be bad news. They could maintain this vow of silence if they insisted, but after what I had witnessed in St Moritz I could almost hear Beatriz whispering Felix's grades and George's fury echoing off the walls. Then Beatriz walked in.

'Great results, Matt!'

'I . . . when did you find out?'

'Last night.'

'Oh.'

'George isn't satisfied. But he never is.'

The results, when I saw them, weren't as good as Beatriz was making out. But nor were they as bad as I had feared. Felix claimed he wasn't bothered, and I assumed that as usual, his true feelings would remain a mystery. He hadn't been set any homework and was keen to play table football. I was desperate to avoid another sporting humiliation that could be ridiculed by Big Buddy, but I had to admit that Felix deserved a reward.

My performance was as expected. But as we played, Felix chatted freely. I'm not sure if it was the lack of pressure or having the game as a distraction, but we discussed everything from the death of Michael Jackson to the phenomenon of artificial insemination.

'It's funny, isn't it, life?' Felix mused.

Before I knew it, we were talking about his parents. He admitted how much he hated it when they argued, and told me his biggest dream was to move to Australia.

'I want to live on the Great Barrier Reef,' he said earnestly. 'You can get underwater houses made of glass.'

115

I was happy to let him believe it. This was a side of Felix I'd never seen. How many people had he encountered in his life who were only there because his parents were paying them? Maybe it was always going to take a while to earn his trust. Felix, however, had his own idea of what this new spirit of candour meant for our relationship. He looked at me with deep sincerity.

'Do you want to know what I dream when I poo?'

Me: Well? Do you?

Zoe: Matt. I'm eating.

Saturday, 4 July, Wiltshire

'Wow!' said my aunt. 'Sounds like you've had a fun year.'

I had come to a village hall near Swindon for a family gathering, and couldn't deny my aunt's assessment considering that I had just regaled her with the story of my trip in a private jet. When I put it all together and left out the parts about my love life and my writing career, it did sound quite fun. I was a little less buoyant getting my parents up to speed. They had heard my tutoring tales already, which meant my only news was Amanda's damning assessment of my script.

'It's only one person,' said my mum.

'I'm sure someone else will like it,' said my dad.

'Did I tell you my new neighbour is a man with a wooden leg?' said my granny. 'He served me an enormous bit of cake with a teaspoon! But he's very nice.'

It wasn't hard to see why my first attempt at writing a screenplay had been a heartwarming comedy set in the fictional town of Piddle Newton. My granny was not even the most eccentric family member present. Great Uncle Mike was visiting England from the village in rural Mexico he had made his home for the past forty years. He chatted about the new ox his neighbour Casildo had bought, then boasted of the solar-powered cooker he had invented which was capable of boiling beans in only twenty-four hours. I had always drawn comfort from Uncle Mike's presence in the family. Most of my relatives had taken the more familiar path of a middle class profession. But when Mike had gone off on a tangent none of us could have predicted, nobody had said a thing.

'And what are you boys doing these days?' asked Uncle Mike.

He was addressing me and my older brother, who like me had embraced the freelance life as a journalist. Mike entertained our updates, while not seeming to understand that we weren't currently looking for jobs.

'Have you thought about starting a business?'

My brother and I shared a glance.

'What do you mean?'

'In Mexico they sell juice in these little metallic boxes. Imagine the fortune you could make if you introduced them to Europe.'

117

'Boxes of juice? Like a juice box?'

'That's a good name for it,' said Uncle Mike. 'A juice box.'

Hi Matt,
Can you give me a call?
I might have something for you . . .
    Philippa

Me: FUCK
Zoe: What?!

MOSCOW

I wasn't meant to be travelling to the oligarch's house by bus. It had all started out so promisingly when I arrived at the airport the previous day to find a chauffeur waiting. Oleg was a stocky man with a dense fringe and a card bearing my name. As I approached him, smiling and pointing at the card, he betrayed no visible reaction but turned and walked towards the car park. An hour later, he had transported me to a rented apartment in an upscale city neighbourhood and his face had still not registered a single emotion, nor his fringe moved a millimetre.

'Thank you so much,' I said. 'What time are you coming tomorrow?'

'Yes,' Oleg said.

The following morning, I had been waiting for half an hour where Oleg left me when I began to accept that he wasn't coming. It was about the first chance I'd had to catch my breath since Philippa had let me know about a last-minute gig for a boy applying to English boarding school. The original tutor had got a job offer from Goldman Sachs, and for the second time in my career I was going up a gear by stepping into someone else's shoes. I had even been transferred the original tutor's flights. But the smooth operation had ended there. Not only had Oleg gone AWOL, my phone hadn't worked since landing. Luckily I had the client's address written down. I approached a plump, middle-aged woman standing by the side of the road and pointed at the address. She stared at it as though it was written in hieroglyphs. Then I realised it might as well have been. I made my best attempt to sound it out.

'Rublyovka,' the woman said with a look of foreboding, as though we were in Middle Earth and I had announced my intention to head to Mordor. After pointing me towards the correct bus, she silenced my panicked enquiries about how to pay by giving me a shiny coin for my fare.

The bus was crowded and, a few stops in, a sweaty man in a bomber jacket got on and sat next to me, mumbling something as he did. Not having any idea what he had said, I smiled. The man glared at me as though I had blown him a kiss. I was suddenly very aware of the danger of having zero communication skills in a country that wasn't exactly gay-friendly. I had already planned to stay firmly in the closet for the duration of my trip. Now I felt nothing less than total deadpan would suffice.

Half an hour later, the outskirts of Moscow had given way to pine forest and I was starting to worry I had boarded the wrong bus. I tried to recall what the sweaty man had said when he got on, which I now felt sure was

Russian for 'Is this the bus to take the potato pickers to Siberia?' I had no capacity to confirm or deny this, not unless I resorted to mime. Then I heard it — as mystical and mysterious as the woman had made it sound — *Rublyovka*. Leaping up as if someone had said the safe word at a disappointing orgy, I jumped off the bus and left the potato pickers to continue to their icy destination.

As I walked off the main road, it hardly felt like I had arrived in the land of oligarchs. All I could see were fences. The land was newly developed, each compound linked by a plonked-down strip of tarmac and unlit dirt tracks which gave the area a vaguely feudal feel. Maybe that's what they were going for. I reached the client's address — a modern mansion with an extraordinary stuccoed façade, its key architectural influences seemingly art deco, marzipan and the Teletubbies. As I was buzzed through the gate, a creature came bounding towards me. It was an extremely large dog, but had neither ears nor tail, and was leaking saliva from its gums by the gallon.

'Miätt?'

I looked up to see a glamorous woman in her late thirties standing on the porch, cradling a Yorkshire terrier like a handbag. I presumed this was my pupil's mother Maria, though it was hard to confirm on account of the giant dog that was now sniffing around my groin and depositing large patches of spit.

'We cut off ear and tail,' Maria said breezily, 'so wolf cannot bite.'

Wait, *wolf?* Of all the risks I had associated with taking a job in Moscow, being bitten by a wolf was not one of them. As Maria invited me inside, the dog tried to follow me in, but Maria shut the door on him.

'He never comes in house,' she said with a smile. 'Outside dog.'

Inside, Maria introduced me to her terrier Dolly, with whom she shared a matching red nail manicure and an impressive blonde coiffure. Dolly was certainly living the life compared to Outside Dog. I told Maria the issue with my phone, suggesting I might need a new SIM card. 'No, Miätt,' Maria said. 'Oleg will get you new phone.'

The issue of how I had arrived at the house and whose fault it had been did not trouble Maria, who I guessed lived above such matters. She was far more interested in giving me a tour. The house had been newly built to the family's own design, the proportions so big they had run out of ideas for filling the space. Maria announced each room's function on entering — bedroom, bathroom etc. But slowly the announcements tailed off. One room contained nothing but a putting machine and a grandfather clock. Another housed a punchbag, an ultrasonic humidifier and a large painting of an apple. In the kitchen, Maria seemed uncertain of its basic layout. She handed me a light-up electronic mouse on a rod and string and pointed to her cat. 'Yes please,' she said.

There was no reason not to think that, due to a miscommunication, I had been flown to Russia for a month to play with an oligarch's cat. But eventually Maria remembered that she had a son. He was in the basement, playing a game on a full replica go-kart, the sort you'd happily blow 50p on in a Bournemouth amusement arcade. He had a placid but dutiful demeanour and looked uncommonly clean for a ten-year-old, with long, straight hair that glowed with the sheen of an international brand ambassador.

'This is Nicky,' Maria said.

'I am Nicky,' he repeated uncertainly.

'Nikita?' I said, which was the name the agency had given me.

'Nikita is a girl's name.'

'So is Nicky!'

'Nicky' looked appalled. It turned out that someone at the agency had suggested Nikita might be better off using an anglicised form of his name if he was planning to go to school in England. I tried explaining the nuances of the various options, but in the ensuing confusion Maria became convinced that the ideal way to refer to her son was 'Nicholas Nick'. Nicholas Nick looked alarmed. I noticed he was wearing a Manchester United shirt, and decided some generic football-related comment would put him at ease.

'Ah,' I said. 'Man United.'

'No,' said Nicholas Nick politely. 'Liverpool.'

Zoe:	How is it?
Zoe:	Matt???
Zoe:	These aren't delivering
Zoe:	Helloooooooooo?

That night, we drove into the city to meet Maria's husband for dinner. I had visions of Red Square and that cathedral with the domes, but we stopped while we were still on the outskirts. The restaurant's exterior gave nothing away. Inside, Russia's answer to Laurence Llewelyn-Bowen had been allowed to run riot. Appliqué silver swirls adorned the walls, while a centrepiece fountain got diners in the mood with what can only be described as an eternally vomiting swan. Maria turned to me excitedly.

'Do you like it?'

'Mmm.'

'Good. You can come here whenever you want and eat what you like, because . . . we own it!'

As we were shown to our table, Maria explained that the restaurant scene in Moscow was ruined by traffic jams that clogged up the city every night. Rather than put up with the hassle, they had simply found a more convenient location, installed a chef and decor to their liking, and now had a bespoke restaurant experience at their disposal. When the cost was irrelevant, it made perfect sense.

Sergei was waiting for us on the other side of the room. Maria had proudly trailed him as Russia's leading producer of milk, making him sound like some great-teated beast. Having pictured him with enormous breasts being milked at a furious rate, I was disappointed to find that he more closely resembled the publicity-shy husband of the first female prime minister of a minor Baltic nation.

'Welcome,' he said. 'We love British.'

'Is true!' said Maria. 'Range Rover. Bentley. Yorkshire terrier.'

'Did you already met her?' said Sergei.

I looked confused, then realised he was referring not to his wife but her dog. They weren't just listing brands, but their personal inventory.

'And you,' Sergei said. 'You went to Cambridge.'

Philippa had made it clear from the start that my degree was a powerful brand in the tutoring world, but out here it had reached the status of designer label. I answered Sergei's questions about my time there, but he got a little lost in my explanation of the college system and I realised I needed to speak his language.

'It's sort of like . . . Harry Potter!'

The family burst out laughing, repeating my claim ad nauseam. I was relieved — after a year of trying to master the fine grain class distinctions of individual London postcodes, it looked as if out here I was going to be able to paint with a slightly broader brush. If this was all it took, perhaps I could become a famed raconteur among the Moscow elite by jauntily reciting the words 'Marmite' or 'Paddington Bear'. On the other hand, Philippa had warned me that my success at this job hinged on my ability to deliver another internationally famous British brand to the Kerzakhovs — one of the few that money alone couldn't buy.

'So,' said Sergei, suddenly nervous. 'How can we make place in Eton?'

*

I can't say I had any idea how to make place in Eton. I would never have got this job if Philippa hadn't needed to parachute in a graduate of Harry Potter University at the last minute. Thankfully, Nicholas Nick was the best student I had ever taught. He combined impeccable precision with incredible diligence. Each time he made a mistake, he made a neat little note in a perfectly ordered journal. The thought that Nicholas Nick might one day come up against the likes of Horace and Felix in the corridors of power made me geopolitically nervous for my nation. The only kink in his armour came in his eagerness to employ English idioms. In our first lesson, he dropped a pen on the floor.

'Oopsy daisy lemon squeaky!' he exclaimed.

Nicholas Nick would not be taking the test until the following autumn, meaning the pressure was well and truly off. After my exertions with Felix, I couldn't believe my luck and looked forward to a month of freewheeling — not least since I had just been handed a fully functioning iPhone. But Maria had no intention of getting such little bang for her buck. Sergei worked very long hours, meaning I had dinner most nights at home with Nicholas Nick and Maria. She insisted I sat at the head of the table and personally served me whatever the housekeeper had cooked up. It was already fairly on the nose as a simulacrum of the family unit. Then one day, Nicholas Nick's enthusiasm for second helpings earned him the nickname Little Piggy. It was only a matter of time before our dynamic was formalised by the christening of Mummy Piggy and Daddy Piggy.

Zoe: !!!!!!!!!!!!!!!

From then on, the Piggies went from strength to strength. I got the sense that Maria wanted me to be everything her husband was not — above all, an entertainer. She taught me basic Russian phrases which I parroted back like an obliging cockatoo, repeating them on command until their entertainment value had been comprehensively exhausted. Once Daddy Piggy understood his role, the performances became more elaborate. One night, I turned a tea towel into a nun's habit and gave a full rendition of 'How Do You Solve A Problem Like Maria?' Maria wasn't familiar with the song and appeared to think I had improvised an original number about her.

'Very clever piggy!' she declared.

I had never had anything but disdain for the cult of the patriarch. Now that I had been installed as one, it was hard not to see the benefits. I was all set to enjoy my reign when the next night, Sergei made it home in time for dinner. Towards the end of the meal, Maria asked who wanted the final dumpling.

'You have it, Daddy Piggy,' Nicholas Nick said to me with a smile.

Sergei stared at me. Maria froze. But as Nicholas Nick innocently explained our nicknames, Sergei wasn't angry, merely bemused. Nevertheless, we all understood that whenever Sergei was home, our Piggy names were not to be used.

Zoe: You'll always be Daddy Piggy to me

Maria had just opened a beauty salon, of which she proudly described herself as the CEO. It was a joint venture with her best friend Nina, a large, jolly woman who acted like Maria's lady-in-waiting. Nina came over for frequent 'business meetings' which tended to involve Nina giving Maria a massage or a manicure, no doubt in the name of research and development. Since Nina rarely crossed paths with Sergei, she was a natural addition to the Piggy family. Before long, her enviable figure had earned her the nickname Titty Piggy.

'Titty Piggy can make you lovely feet,' said Maria, which was a claim that was going to require some explanation. Instead, she asked if I wanted to visit the salon. It was located in an industrial part of Moscow off a roundabout — a district of strip lighting and tacky fonts, until you arrived at Skin Deep Hair and Beauty. The sign was in English, which was the first clue you had come to a classy joint. Inside, a waiting area had fully embraced the possibilities of fuchsia pleather, though there was no sign of any paying customers. Maria showed me round the various rooms, listing the treatments on offer.

'You can have eyebrow waxed . . . you can have wart removed . . .'

She made it sound like I was being offered the treatments personally, and I started to worry this was indeed her plan, and I would leave here with collagen injections and a Brazilian butt lift. But Maria had not forgotten what I had been promised. As Titty Piggy gave me one of her famous pedicures, Maria took photos — whether for promotional purposes or her personal collection I felt no need to clarify.

My trip to the salon was the talk of dinner that night. As before, Sergei did not seem annoyed, merely intrigued that his wife was extracting such value from their latest British toy. Until now, he had not shown any interest in getting to know me. But at the end of the meal, he asked if I wanted to go for a drive in the Bentley.

Maria and Nicholas Nick were as surprised as I was. But there was no question of declining Sergei's invitation. As we set out into the night, Sergei began to narrate the journey. His dull monotone wouldn't score him any rave reviews on Yelp, but his local knowledge illuminated the properties beyond the fences that shielded them. He pointed towards one sprawling construction.

'That is house . . . behind, swimming pool . . . behind, helipad!'

Suddenly the topography was horribly clear. A minute or so later, we passed another compound and Sergei told me the name of the person who lived there and chuckled to himself. I looked blank.

'It's funny because he's a terrorist.'

'Ha ha,' I said.

We had reached the end of the neighbourhood and were driving out of Rublyovka and onto an empty freeway. There was no indication that Sergei had a destination in mind, or that he had thought through our excursion beyond this point. But it was too soon to turn round without admitting it had been a flop. I wracked my brains for a conversation topic.

'Maria said you're one of the biggest milk producers in Russia.'

'Yes.'

'How do you produce so much?'

'Cows.'

'Yes—'

'Four million.'

'Wow.'

That felt as much as I ever needed to know about dairy production in the former Soviet Union. Luckily Sergei was in a similar mood and headed towards home. When we got there, Maria and Nicholas Nick had gone to bed and I couldn't have been any keener to join them. But Sergei was not done yet.

'Come,' he said. 'It's a tradition.'

The last time a client had said this, a personal chef had escorted me and my sledge up and down a mountain. I couldn't say I wasn't intrigued to learn what late night traditions the Russian super-rich enjoyed.

'Pork fat,' Sergei grinned.

He explained that the tradition was to consume slices of fat with shots of vodka, then led me to the kitchen and pulled the essentials from the fridge. The pork fat was surprisingly delicious. But the vodka proved no lubricant to our non-existent chemistry. After a while, Sergei admitted defeat and turned on MTV, where we were greeted by the sight of Jennifer Lopez.

'She has big ass,' said Sergei.

We waited in silence for the next song to begin. I wondered how Sergei felt about gay people, and what might happen if Ricky Martin appeared on screen, hips thrusting. Thankfully it was Jay-Z.

'I had dinner with Lenny Kravitz once,' Sergei said. 'And Cindy Crawford. She is forty-five, good-looking. She has also Damien Hirst.'

The following morning our boys' night was firmly behind us, which meant it could be spun as a success. Maria was sweetly amused, perhaps knowing her husband could never compete with her skills as a hostess. A few days later she gave me a wink.

'Tonight, we will do karaoke.'

I tended to remain oblivious to any instances of female interest, but over the course of the month Maria had become progressively more tactile, while expressing incredulity that I didn't have a girlfriend. This was not helped by Zoe texting lurid speculation about what she imagined Maria doing upstairs with her photos from the salon. I couldn't help but wonder — when Sergei wasn't around, how far did Daddy Piggy's duties extend?

That night, Maria drove us to famed Moscow karaoke joint Who Is Who. The club was empty when we arrived, and as Maria ordered cocktails, I assumed we would work our way up to some drunken singing. But Maria wanted entertaining straight away. Perhaps I could do something bouncy and slightly camp.

'"I'm Yours",' Maria beamed.

I got up and sang with as much detachment as you can get away with when you are performing to a woman who pays your wages and has requested a song whose lyrics mark you as her property. Maria clapped vigorously then went to the bathroom, and I became convinced she was preparing to make her move. I rehearsed potential excuses, from professionalism to morality, and the last resort of my sexuality.

But as Maria got back from the bathroom, there was a commotion. Someone had entered the club who caused everyone to take notice — a Russian pop star, accompanied by an entourage and dressed in a studded leather jacket and cowboy boots. People began calling for him to sing. At first the star feigned disinterest. But there was a reason he had come to famed Moscow karaoke joint Who Is Who. Before long, he got up to perform one of his hits. The crowd went wild.

'Is OK,' said Maria with a shrug.

Already, people were clamouring for the star to do another number. He laughed and shook his head in a way which left no doubt he'd be back up there soon. Maria turned to me with an urgent look.

'James Blunt.' She made it sound like the code word for some emergency police procedure. '*James. Blunt.* Go on!'

I knew what I had to do. 'You're Beautiful' had been a hit around the world, but it had struck a particular chord in Russia. I had promised Maria I would perform it and she had been saving it for the night's climax. Now the stakes were higher than she could have dreamed. No one had dared follow the pop star, and as I got up on stage, people looked at me like I was mad. But Maria was full of belief. As I started to sing, the room gasped in recognition. One very drunk person clearly thought I *was* James Blunt, and perhaps still does. Some listened in reverent silence, others sang along to the words they knew so well. But no one was happier than Maria. She might have envisaged it as a private performance, but this impromptu Eurovision song contest was more fun than either of us could have dreamed. Maria led the crowd in a standing ovation. Five minutes later, the pop star got up and left.

Daddy Piggy had taken Moscow. But Mummy Piggy was too drunk to drive home. Maria called a service which promptly delivered two men to the club. One took Maria's keys from her while the other took us to his car. You had to hand it to the rich for continually coming up with these ways to make their lives even easier.

'I'm so tired,' Maria said as we bundled into the back seat of our escort vehicle. Since the taxi service had not yet hit upon the idea of fitting beds in the back of their cars, Maria collapsed her head onto my lap. To give her credit, it was the closest a woman has ever got to my sexual organs. But I'm not convinced Maria had planned a seduction. She was guided less by strategy than an instinctive sense of how I could serve her in the moment, which right then was as a human cushion. Even now, she was dreaming of new ways to make the most of me. She drifted asleep, then opened her eyes and gazed up hazily.

'Next time, we do conversation lessons. Just you and me, on some island. Maybe Bali?'

Zoe: Matt, I am not kidding – you have found
             the one

A few days later, I ended up in the basement with a naked Sergei. I had got used to taking a sauna after lessons, often with Nicholas Nick but never wearing anything less than a pair of trunks. Sergei had kept his distance since the night of the pork fat, so I had been surprised when he had suggested a traditional *banya*. But if he was bothered by my refusal to adhere to traditional *banya* attire, he hid it well. It was only when he offered to spank me that I started to wonder about his motivations. Did he see this as an exercise in bonding or domination? Maybe he had sat back and watched me befriend his wife, waiting only to see how many strikes of the birch branch my behaviour would accrue. But it seemed equally possible that the spanking was benevolent, and that given our lack of chemistry, such a ritual was the closest we would ever get to connecting. Either way, my month in Russia had honed my instincts for client satisfaction. I bent over and let Sergei spank me as much as he liked.

The day before I was due to leave, Maria drove me and Nicholas Nick to the local park. We arrived at a spot with a view over the city, and Maria led us to a bench scrawled in permanent marker with sweet nothings from teenage lovers.

'For lovelies,' Maria said.

We sat and watched the sun set while local youths strolled about holding hands and drinking from plastic bottles of beer. I couldn't imagine this was typical behaviour for an oligarch's wife, and wondered if the restaurant and salon which Maria had set up for herself on the outskirts of town were really a matter of convenience, or a sign that she felt more comfortable there than among the city's elite.

'Matt, I make you gift,' said Maria. 'I design myself. Special for you.'

She reached for her bag and handed me a wrapped package. It contained a customised silk cushion printed with a photo of Dolly, her Yorkshire terrier. It was a studio shot, the dog's coat impeccably styled, her head topped with a red bow. Beneath the photo were printed the words 'From Russia With Love'.

SCOTLAND

My pay cheque from Moscow was far more money than I'd ever made. In London it was hard to earn more than an hour at a time, but in Russia I got paid for four hours a day whether I taught them or not, and had zero expenses for a month. For the first time in memory, I had money to spare. There was no question of doing anything sensible like saving it, but with most of the summer gone, my options were limited. Then I read an article about a travelling film festival organised by Tilda Swinton. This felt like it must be a joke, or at least an art project from someone at Goldsmiths. But no — there was a website inviting people to spend a week accompanying a mobile cinema from one side of Scotland to the other. Once you bought your ticket, there Tilda was, signing her name on an email which combined Robert Bresson quotes with some useful info on where you could get dinner in Inverness for under a tenner.

'I just got an email from Tilda Swinton,' I announced to my mum.

137

'That's nice,' said my mum. 'I got one from Johnnie Boden.'

I had come home to Dorset to steal my parents' camping equipment. They were happy to lend a tent, but my mum was holding out on her favourite cooking pot because she had memories of her own mother using it to make bread sauce. I didn't see why that meant I couldn't create further memories by using it to heat up some bean soup for Academy Award Winner Tilda Swinton. For some reason, my parents weren't as excited about my impending encounter with a film star as I was.

From Dorset I caught two trains and a coach to the Scottish Highlands. Arriving at our meeting point, it wasn't hard to spot the Oscar-winning actress among the gaggle of cinephiles in anoraks. She had a bleach blonde crop and an aura which made it hard not to stare. Now that I was in her presence, I had to get her attention. I got chatting to an Irish guy who had come on the trip with the express purpose of getting Tilda to read his short film script. When he asked what I did, I said something vague about writing and teaching. My rejection call from Amanda transformed into a screenplay I had in development with an acclaimed director. What if everyone here was an aspiring filmmaker? I excused myself from the Irishman and got talking to a friendly American woman in a straw bonnet.

'Big fan of Tilda,' she said chirpily. 'But not her films. I used to role play on MySpace as the White Witch's bald servant.'

As the pilgrimage got under way, I found someone else diverting my attention. Among my fellow travellers was a guy my age called Peter. He was a pint-sized, baby-faced Canadian film journalist — all information I knew not because he told me, but because before arriving in Scotland I had spotted him in a Facebook group for festival attendees and forced Zoe to have several serious discussions about whether he was more likely to be my husband or a summer fling. Both of these options were put on the back burner when I found out that Peter was already hooking up with a German student called Toby. My romantic reveries were permanently forgotten as the three of us got to know each other and rapidly became friends. Each time we reached a new town we would gather in the back of the mobile cinema to giggle our way through that night's film with a box of wine, then head out to sit in a field or by a loch and talk into the night.

'That film gave me PTSD,' said Peter. 'The villain reminded me of this straight guy who made me call him Daddy while I sat on his face.'

I'll leave you to imagine what Toby was reminded of when we stopped in Fort Augustus for battered sausage. In three years at Cambridge, I had never met anyone so comfortable recounting such wild experiences. I was rapt.

'So what are the men like in London?' Toby asked me one evening.

I wasn't sure I was the best person to answer. Since moving to London I had been to the odd gay bar, but somehow being closeted at work had trickled into my private life. My handful of half-hearted encounters were no match for the scandalous adventures of my fabulous new gay friends.

'God,' I said to Toby. 'Don't get me started.'

The week passed in a blur. Whole towns came and went before I could learn their names. I was a different person around Toby and Peter. I think the technical term is 'gaying it up'. I cracked jokes about sex acts I'd never even attempted. But it didn't feel like faking it. I felt more at ease than I ever had in London or Cambridge. Why couldn't I be like this all the time?

'Did you meet that guy who's trying to get Tilda his screenplay?' said Toby one day. 'That's not what this trip is about.'

'No,' I said. 'It's really not.'

On our last night, we gathered on the beach with as much supermarket vodka as we could carry and stayed there until sunrise. The following day, I stumbled into town to catch my train home. The preceding seven days had been a perfect storm of dodgy signal and dead battery, and it was the first time I'd had contact with the outside world all week. I immediately texted Zoe.

OMG, last night I went skinny dipping with Tilda then had a four way kiss on the beach with my Scottish lover, Dustin Lance Black's ex and a German model.

None of this was technically true. Neither myself nor the Academy Award Winner in our midst had gone naked for our midnight swim, Toby was very attractive but not a model, Peter had only had a one night stand with the man in question, and 'my Scottish lover' was a local youth who had got roped into proceedings after one too many swigs of value whisky. But up here I saw everything through rose-tinted spectacles. I wasn't some bumbling tutor whose private life barely merited a PG certificate, but a liberated young writer revelling in his freedoms. Unfortunately my trip had come to an end and I already had clients lined up for the new academic year. There was no doubt which version of myself they would be meeting. The question was how long I could keep up the act.

YEAR TWO

AUTUMN TERM 2009

NEW JOB ALERT

Job number: 4417

What: Bertie is applying for a place at St Paul's. His mother Jocasta would like to meet prospective candidates for coffee at Electric House.

Where: Notting Hill

When: Thursdays, 4 p.m.

Tuesday, 8 September, Notting Hill

Before I was even back in the country, Philippa had emailed to tell me there was a big demand for experienced tutors at the start of the school year. It was not a descriptor I would have applied to myself, not least since I had decided to switch my focus from study buddying to entrance test preparation. I hoped this would bring a little more purpose to proceedings, not to mention some of the perks that the Kerzakhovs had been prepared to

145

fund in pursuit of their goal. Early signs were promising when I looked up Electric House and discovered that it was a branch of Soho House, a members' club for creative professionals. A further google revealed that Jocasta was some sort of fashion stylist and a fixture on London's party scene. She was no longer a prospective client. She was a potential new best friend.

I wouldn't have had such thoughts had it not been for Maria. She had shown that my key client relationship could just as easily be the parent as the child. Jocasta might lead a glamorous life, but maybe she would find someone like me refreshing. Slowly she would come to trust my judgement and abandon her inner circle in favour of flying me to Milan Fashion Week to get my thoughts on the new Raf Simons collection. I found her seated at the Electric House bar, browsing a trade magazine and sipping a latte I presumed wasn't cow's milk. She had a cascade of wavy brown hair and a blue leather jacket which I guessed had a cute little back story involving a side street in Covent Garden and a hot young designer who Jocasta had been tracking since his graduation show at St Martin's.

'You don't mind doing this, do you?' said Jocasta as I took a seat. 'Bertie's last tutor was all wrong.'

I wanted to tell her how little I minded being summoned to meet a woman who had only recently been photographed in the company of Vivienne Westwood, but I knew I should play it cool. Maybe that's where Bertie's last tutor went wrong.

'Admissions are a nightmare these days,' Jocasta lamented. 'The anxiety, the in-fighting, the obsession with reports.'

'Oh god,' I said. 'Total nightmare.'

'So what's your trick for getting into St Paul's?'

I paused and gave her a coy smile, as though I wasn't going to give up my secrets that easily. Philippa might be relaxed about throwing me into the crowded entrance test market, but my experience in Moscow hardly made me an expert.

'My parents are teachers,' I said, thinking this would garnish whatever bullshit I was about to invent with a hint of authority, 'and apparently these days it's all about the interview.'

Jocasta leaned forward as if I was some sort of soothsayer.

'I'm not saying it's *not* about the tests,' I continued, covering my bases carefully. 'But the interview is the place where a lot of people fall down.'

When you looked at it, I was saying almost nothing. But I had convinced Jocasta. She launched into a stream-of-consciousness portrait of her son while I nodded along sympathetically. I had become distracted by an actor on the other side of the room who I was sure I had seen on TV playing second fiddle to Tamzin Outhwaite.

'Glad you agree,' said Jocasta, though I have no idea what with. 'I think you'll be a perfect fit for Bertie.'

I assured her I would, wishing I had listened a little more carefully to what had been said about this boy I had just claimed as my kindred spirit. Jocasta glanced at her phone and said she needed to make a move. I suddenly wondered if she had been performing her own sly seduction and the joke was on me for taking on another nightmare pupil. She looked across the room, her mind already elsewhere. Why did I think she would ever be interested in me? I'd probably get fobbed off on the nanny and never speak to her again.

I looked up to see the actor I recognised striding towards us.

'Tobias,' Jocasta said casually. 'Meet my friend Matt.'

Beatriz: Can you come early tomorrow Matt? We'd like a quick chat about Felix x

Saturday, 12 September, Highgate

'I'm a St Paul's man,' said George. 'That's where Northover men go.'

Felix looked like he wanted the ground to swallow him. I let go of any hopes that a summer on the Northovers' private ranch in Kenya had somehow transformed his attitude towards his studies. St Paul's was widely regarded as London's top boys' school, so it was no surprise that it was two of my clients' first choice. But my meeting with Jocasta had felt like a novelty. If even George would consent to find me five minutes, maybe this whole admissions business was more serious than I thought.

'We just thought it would be a good idea to . . . touch base,' said Beatriz.

'Show him the damn thing,' said George.

Beatriz pulled out a practice paper they had got Felix to do over the summer.

'Oh Matt,' said Beatriz. 'It looks like it was written by a drunk primate.'

I was fairly sure that parenting manuals didn't recommend passing judgements like this in front of your child, but Felix maintained such an implacable expression I almost suspected this was exactly who he had paid to complete the test for him. I examined his effort. To be fair to Felix, it was far beyond the skill set of your average alcoholic baboon. Unfortunately it was hard to be much more complimentary.

'If this is his standard,' said George, 'does he have a shot at St Paul's?'

'He's definitely got a shot.'

That was true even if the odds were one in a million.

'It's so ridiculous what they put them through,' sighed Beatriz.

What the hell did St Paul's do to their applicants? And why had I agreed to take charge of two of them without knowing any of this?

'Is St Paul's the only place he's applying?'

'Yes,' snapped George, standing up from his seat. I wondered if his habit of ending conversations abruptly was something he had ever discussed with a therapist,

149

but figured now was not the time to ask.

'Just make sure you get in,' George said to Felix. 'Otherwise you'll never be motivated to try for anything ever again.'

Zoe: So excited about seeing you later! Text me when you get to the station

Friday, 18 September, Kent

There had to be some consolation to turning the virtually senile age of twenty-four. I considered hosting a party in my self-contained studio flat, until I remembered I'd led half my friends to believe it was basically a penthouse. I thought about asking someone else to host, but the kind of people who had ample living space at our age were not ones I wanted anywhere near my party. Then I hit on a solution — boomers. Zoe's parents were going away, and for some inexplicable reason were happy for us to use their house in Kent. I caught the train down the day before so I could help Zoe with preparations. I wish I could report that we were planning a rave, but for some reason I was set on hosting a dinner party. Rather than cling to my youth, I would convince myself and everyone else that I was now a classy and sophisticated adult.

'Good luck!' said Zoe.

I made a new and firm commitment to cling to my youth at any cost. But that didn't mean our party couldn't be classy and sophisticated. As we drove to the supermarket to stock up on fancy things like napkins, conversation turned to tutoring. Zoe had settled into a groove of teaching A-Level English — a clear brief with obvious stakes. I admitted I was surprised in comparison by how seriously my clients were taking this entrance test preparation.

'Why?' said Zoe. 'It's everything to them.'

'But there are so many schools to choose from.'

'Are you kidding? They wouldn't dream of sending their kids to a *minor* public school.'

I was well aware that not all private schools were created equal. But it was mad to think there were parents who would consider a school like the one I attended, with its theatre and sports centre and leafy grounds, as beyond the pale.

'Somewhere like St Paul's . . . it's more like a university,' explained Zoe. 'You're already ten steps ahead when you get to Oxbridge, then by the time you've graduated, you're ready to rule the world. It's the golden ticket.'

So that was how you explained someone like Nick. He was on my mind again, since shortly after getting back from Scotland I had seen that he had cast a legendary theatre actress in his latest play. It was so easy to go from revelling in my own experience with a famous actress to thinking that every choice I'd ever made was the wrong one and I was never going to make it. I told Zoe how

151

much I preferred the version of myself I was in Scotland.

Zoe was unsurprised. 'Everyone's a different person on holiday.'

If only it were that simple. I admitted I had run out of ideas for writing an Oscar-winning script. Zoe suggested that rather than bang my head against a brick wall, I found something outside writing or tutoring to spark my interest.

'Is this your way of telling me it's going well with the Italian?'

'Yes,' said Zoe. 'But I don't just mean dating. It could be, I don't know, bee-keeping.'

'Fine,' I said. 'As long as it's one of the two.'

Hello Matthew,
Thanks so much for your interest. I'm attaching a form for you to fill in.
Looking forward to meeting you!
    Martin :)

Saturday, 10 October, Waterloo

For a week or two, I hadn't known what to do about Zoe's suggestion. Then I watched the film *Milk* and decided it was time to do my part for gay liberation. In the film, Harvey Milk was inspired to a life of activism by hitting forty and deciding he hadn't done a thing he was proud of. I wasn't quite at that stage. But it had been a while since I participated in my school volunteer programme performing unrehearsed selections from *The Best of Gilbert and Sullivan* in old people's homes. Even then, I had only done it to get out of rugby.

I emailed the country's leading LGBT charity to see if they had any opportunities for volunteering. Having made substantial progress as a nation since the Buggery Act of 1533, the charity's focus was now on school and workplace homophobia. I was put in touch with a man called Martin, who suggested the role of youth mentor, supporting teenagers as they mounted anti-bullying campaigns in their schools and colleges. Martin invited me in for a chat to learn more.

The charity's headquarters were on the tenth floor of a high rise overlooking the Thames. Walking in, I felt like I was on safari. Apart from a single week's temping, my idea of what it was like to work in an office came entirely from films and TV. Maybe this is what I had been missing — sitting down at a desk with my name on it and having a clear sense of purpose. Not that I had the slightest idea what any of these jobs entailed.

'Thanks for coming in,' said Martin. 'Did you bring the form I sent you?'

'Shit.'

Martin smiled. He was round and cheery and the kind of person who had a large collection of hilarious mugs and knew just the right one to elicit a chuckle when you were having a bad day.

'That's OK,' Martin said, having predicted this exact scenario and pulling out a copy of the form. 'It's just a few questions. We can fill it in now.'

He scanned the piece of paper in front of him.

'Do you have access to email?'

I pulled a face. 'We arranged this meeting over email.'

'I just need to tick the box.'

'Sure. Yes.'

'Great. Any criminal convictions?'

I stared at Martin.

'I take it that's a no.'

'No! I mean yes. It's a no.'

'Great, and finally — are you available on Saturdays?'

'Those are the three questions?'

Martin held up the sheet to prove he wasn't lying.

'I guess most of our volunteer days are Saturdays.'

'I'm available on Saturdays. Did I pass the test?'

Martin gave me a look which suggested that this kind of humour was pushing it for a prospective youth mentor.

'Oh, I forgot about this part,' he said. 'You're meant to write a paragraph on why you want to be a youth mentor.'

I guessed Martin had seen *Milk*, but I wasn't sure if he was ready for me to quote verbatim from Dustin Lance Black's Oscar speech. Now that I thought about it, I wasn't sure if anyone outside Hollywood could pull off describing LGBT youth as 'beautiful, wonderful creatures of value' with a straight face. Was it better to

154

say I wanted to be a mentor because my writing ambitions were on the back burner and no one on Guardian Soulmates was responding to my messages? Somehow I suspected Martin would rather not put that on his form.

'You know what?' said Martin. 'Let's get on with the orientation. You can fill that part out once you've had a think.'

Thursday, 15 October, Notting Hill

I was standing face to face with a stuffed alpaca. Next to that was a faux-marble statue of a Greek philosopher wearing a cowboy hat. On the side, a brass bell was accompanied by a sign which said 'Ring If You Feel Joy'. Under normal circumstances I would have remarked that maybe Joy doesn't want people knowing who she lets finger her. But something about the place defied mockery.

'Would you like a slow gin?' said Jocasta.

'Might have to make it quick one,' I said.

'A *sloe* gin,' Jocasta said, laughing. 'Bertie's late, he's coming from his dad's.'

She showed me into her living room, which was lined floor to ceiling with books. The house was a Bloomsbury fantasy come to life, and becoming Jocasta's new best friend had never felt more urgent. The only bum note was a pug on the end of a chaise longue. Far from lying in graceful repose, the pug had sunk into both the chair and itself, a posture which further impeded its already poor breathing function. It gurgled with each new breath, stopping and starting as if its respiratory passage might clog up completely at any moment. But Jocasta was unconcerned. We heard the front door open.

'Is that you, darling?'

'It's me!' a child's voice warbled. *'I'm Cathy, I've come home!'*

Jocasta turned to me. 'You see what I mean?'

I wasn't sure I did, having zoned out at the crucial moment during our previous meeting. But if what Jocasta had told me was that her son was the kind of person who drops Kate Bush samples into everyday conversation, we weren't going to have a problem. Bertie was eleven, with a natural elegance that was at once childlike and beyond his years. As he looked at me, he flicked his fringe several times, as if he had perfected its ideal configuration through hours of carefully studying the films of Zac Efron. I felt like I understood him already. Jocasta asked Bertie if his father had given him a snack, seeming delighted to learn that he hadn't.

'Go and have a quick bite to eat. Otherwise you'll be an absolute nightmare for poor old Matt.'

'Fine,' said Bertie. 'But we'd *better* not be out of focaccia.'

Fearing this unthinkable eventuality, Jocasta and I followed Bertie to the kitchen, where I watched him assemble a shop-quality focaccia sandwich with terrifying skill.

'You can add that to his list of talents,' Jocasta said admiringly. 'He's always been a good cook.'

Bertie looked at me with a wry smile.

'I'm *so* fabulous.'

I saw no grounds to query this assessment. I would like to say he reminded me of me at his age, but it was a fantasy to think I had ever been so self-assured. This is not to say that Bertie hadn't sensed a certain affinity. Ten minutes into our lesson, he affected a nonchalant look.

'Do you have a girlfriend?'

'No.'

'Why are you smiling?'

'I'm not!'

I encouraged him to focus on his studies. But Bertie proved as good a student as Nicholas Nick, answering every question I put to him and having the syllabus memorised. Bored of his own brilliance, he began responding in a perfect Texas drawl. Soon he was serving full-throated impersonations of what appeared to be a wealthy and sexually rapacious American socialite.

'Kevin was sweet, and Steve — what a doll,' Bertie intoned. 'But I left my heart in South Hampton with a chocolate magnate called Bill.'

At the end of the lesson, I couldn't resist telling Jocasta that this was going to be a far easier task than another client of mine who was aiming for St Paul's from the same prep school.

'Not Beatriz Northover?' said Jocasta.

I admitted that was exactly who I had in mind.

'I know her well,' said Jocasta without the vaguest glimmer of affection. 'Bertie and Felix are great friends.'

Wednesday, 21 October, Hampshire

'No we're not,' said Felix. 'He's so gay.'

'Felix!' said Beatriz. 'Bertie is a lovely boy.'

Beatriz had come to collect me from the station with Felix in tow. They were staying at their country house for half term, a place I had secretly been hoping to visit since tracking it down on Google Images. Now the impending entrance test meant that a week could not be wasted. The Northovers had a driver (I had realised the word 'chauffeur' was terribly common) who took them everywhere in London, but as we entered the gate of their property and proceeded down the driveway, it felt like Beatriz was the Queen at Balmoral, just wanting to feel normal for a moment. Though there was nothing normal about the length of the driveway, which went on and on and on.

'Here we are!' said Beatriz eventually.

As we turned a corner, an enormous manor house came into view. It had clearly been conceived as a wow moment by whichever duke or count had first built it, but I was learning not to react to this sort of thing. The Kerzakhovs might like me to be impressed by the spoils of their wealth, but Beatriz wanted me to pretend this was any old home. What she couldn't hide her excitement over was the day's big event and the estate's pride and joy — a pheasant shoot.

'Felix can miss the first drive, but NOT the second,' Beatriz said. 'So when you've done an hour, Biff will whip you down in the cart.'

It sounded like a maths problem invented by Jacob Rees-Mogg, but I assumed that when Biff was ready to whip me, I'd know. Before then, Felix had some real problems to solve. The first stage of the admissions process was a pre-test focused on verbal and non-verbal reasoning. The idea of testing reasoning was that it revealed a candidate's innate ability, since it supposedly couldn't be prepared for. The private tutoring industry begged to differ.

'OK,' I said to Felix. 'See if you can crack this. Five people live in a block of flats. Amy lives between John and Mary. Sarah lives on the ground floor. Susan is below Mary. John lives in flat 5. Who lives in flat 4?'

'Mary.'

'No.'

'Susan.'

'No.'

'Paul.'

'There isn't even one called Paul.'

I tried to get Felix to see that it wasn't a question that could be answered without careful consideration. It certainly couldn't be answered when the only thing on your mind was pheasant. At eleven o'clock sharp Felix stood up abruptly, the traditional pheasant shoot schedule wired into his body clock. Biff was a grumpy caretaker who was waiting for us in the golf cart. I had so much respect for any staff who dared to be openly grumpy on the job. I wondered if Biff's real name was Terry and he had been assigned his nickname against his will. At first he ignored my efforts to make small talk. But once he learned I was an employee and not part of the shoot, we were best friends.

'Five grand these people pay for a weekend!' Biff scoffed, not seeming to care if Felix was listening. 'You know what they pay my son? Thirty quid.'

'What does your son do?'

'He's a beater.'

'A beater?'

'Yeah. For the birds.'

I realised how little I knew about pheasant shoots, and started to worry this was going to be more violent than anticipated. But there was no time for any more questions, as we had caught up with the shoot. George and Beatriz were leading a party of ten or twelve, all smiling and chatting while happily brandishing guns. Beatriz looked so delighted with hers that I wondered if she was planning to take out her husband while his back was turned.

'Cheers, Biffo!' called George as he saw us coming.

Biff looked very much like 'Biffo' was where he drew the line, and that he could be counted on to bury the body should Beatriz feel moved to enact her plan. As we joined the group I stood out like a sore thumb, but I couldn't imagine ever wearing so much Barbour outside of a costume party. A man in tweed pantaloons peered at me as if he recognised me from somewhere.

'Are you a Suffolk?'

'No, I'm a Dorset,' I wanted to reply.

'Quick, Felix!' said Beatriz. 'You haven't got long.'

A man in a flat cap gave a signal via walkie-talkie. There were more staff everywhere I looked. Through the trees, several men advanced towards us while aggressively waving white flags which clipped the air noisily. As birds flew up one by one, I thought I understood what beating was, but the visual impression was that the men were surrendering, having decided it wasn't worth being paid £30 to get shot at.

'Come on, Felix!' cried George.

Everyone held back as Felix was granted exclusive rights to fire. Judging by some of the party's reactions this wasn't protocol, except that protocol appeared to be that young master was bloody well going to kill a pheasant. As I watched Felix propel tiny metal canisters towards the birds his parents paid a small army of staff to maintain, I wondered what was going through his mind. Did he care about making a kill, or was he firing out bullets with as little aim and interest as he did revision answers?

Before long there was a flurry of feathers. I watched as a pheasant came tumbling to earth, then realised to my horror that its aerodynamic trajectory was not what Key Stage 3 physics would have you believe, and the bird was hurtling straight towards me. I dived out of its way, almost clattering into Biff and his golf cart. The pheasant landed a few feet from me and flapped about madly until a dog ran up and began to maul it. Felix stared at the dying bird.

'Lovely!' said Beatriz, turning to me. 'Would you like a go?'

Mum:	How was it?
Dad:	Don't tell us – you can't believe we never took you on a pheasant shoot
Me:	Actually no. I'm quite grateful.

Hello Matthew,
I'm forwarding the details of our session at the weekend.
Hope you're ready to be bowled over!
Martin :)

Monday, 28 October, Finsbury Park

I had convinced Martin to take me on as a youth mentor. I was going to guide and inspire teenagers from across the country who had been selected to serve as ambassadors in the fight against homophobia. But first we had to take them tenpin bowling. I met Martin in front of the bowling alley where he had organised our outing. I wasn't sure what the queer leaders of tomorrow would make of London's most retro entertainment venue, but from the moment I saw them I knew the kids were all right. They strode up with a confidence I could only dream of at their age.

The bowling lanes were busy with couples on giggly first dates, teenagers who were far too drunk to bowl in a straight line and men who strutted like peacocks each time they racked up a strike. As we began to play, I was complimented on my distinctive backspin. The compliments trailed off as everyone observed the hit rate of my distinctively backspun balls. I wasn't sure what I was meant to be doing other than projecting a vague sense of maturity, and was relieved when Martin sent me to order sixteen portions of chips.

At the bar, a girl with a Birmingham accent and a dyed green crop cut introduced herself as Holly.

'Have you started planning your project?' she asked perkily.

'Oh, no,' I said. 'I'm actually a mentor.'

Holly did a double take, which I can only assume had everything to do with my youthful demeanour and nothing at all with my complete lack of natural authority. My answer let me off the hook, since it was her and not me who was required to show any initiative — not that this was a problem for Holly, who started to outline the vision she had for tackling homophobia in her sixth form college.

'I just think it's so important to be visibly queer,' she declared.

I felt like a fraud. What would she say if she knew I was in the closet at work? My tutoring persona was not so much heterosexual as incomplete, since I tended to avoid questions rather than lie outright, and there were other aspects of my personality that I left at the door. At first this had felt like common professional practice, or at least good strategy. But the more I bonded with clients, the more it had begun to feel like deception.

Back over at the bowling lane, Martin saw me returning.

'So how do this lot compare to your rich kids? They as cool as this?'

'Ha! They wish.'

Zoe:	How were the kids?
Me:	Extremely gay
Zoe:	I'm so happy for them

Carolyn: Hello Matt! Long time no see. Are you around? I've got a fun one for you.

Monday, 16 November, North Kensington

It took me a moment to recall who Carolyn was. Saying goodbye to clients could be briefly poignant, but I always forgot about them surprisingly fast. As soon as I remembered, I logged on to Carolyn's blog to catch up on her news. Horace had started his A-Levels, and Carolyn had written a lengthy post complaining that his teachers weren't seeing his potential. I really wasn't sure I wanted to get back in bed with this woman, let alone find out her idea of 'a fun one'. But it turned out she wanted help with her younger son Arthur, and not for anything academic. Maybe it would be a relief from the term's general pressures.

Carolyn opened the door wiping her hands on a Mrs Tiggy-Winkle tea towel.

'Sorry,' she said. 'I'm icing Nigella's log.'

As she began muttering about her icing, complaining that Ocado had substituted her favoured brand of organic chocolate, I couldn't help suspecting that life-long Kensington residents bought their chocolate logs at Fortnum & Mason. Making it yourself was very North Kensington. But it wasn't one of Carolyn's blog readers having this bitchy little thought. It was me. Had I finally become one of them?

'How's Horace?' I asked.

'Thriving,' said Carolyn tersely. 'He's really starting to flourish.'

She led me through to the music room, where Arthur was seated per instruction at the piano stool, his shoulders

165

slumped in pre-emptive defeat. 'Bless him,' Carolyn said. 'He's so keen to get that "Once In Royal" solo.'

The treble solo first verse of 'Once In Royal David's City' is a cultural touchstone among a certain crowd and a rite of passage for many young singers. Despite Carolyn's claim, Arthur did not appear to share her enthusiasm. Having hoped for some respite from the admissions treadmill, I was faced with yet more parental ambition. Carolyn was deep into a monologue on what Arthur had gained from his time in a Gamelan orchestra when my stomach rumbled and she asked if I fancied a slice of Nigella's log. I said yes just to get rid of her.

'Right,' I said to Arthur, budging him off the piano stool. 'Shall we start with some ning-a-nongs?'

Carolyn had requested my help because I had sung in a university choir she had dreams of Arthur joining, but that didn't make me a singing teacher. A ning-a-nong was the only warm-up exercise I could remember, but a good opportunity to find out Arthur's vocal range. It ends a full octave from where it begins, meaning one can start out in rude voice only to dwindle calamitously as the ning-a-nong reveals its full scope. But Arthur was barely audible throughout. It was the kind of volume you use when it's someone's birthday on the next table at a restaurant, and you join in because you're keen to seem jolly, but keep it low because you don't want there to be an embarrassing gap when you get to the part where you don't know their name. Arthur's sotto

166

voce was ideally suited to that situation. Unfortunately, his mother had grander ambitions.

'Shall we try it from the top?' I asked. Arthur hesitated, as if I might change my mind and suggest starting from two-thirds of the way through. I began to play, hoping the familiar melody would inspire him to new heights. Alas, his effort was even more feeble. Arthur's voice was on the verge of breaking, which was no doubt why Carolyn was so hell-bent on making *this* his year. But the more he tried to hide it, the more he was forced to place his raging pubescence on display. I may as well have asked him to stand there and count out his pubic hairs.

I attempted to find another area of focus. Arthur's pronunciation was so affected that he was warping the words out of all comprehension.

'Wah a mah-ther,' he sang.

'Try and get that vowel sound right. *Where* a *mother*—'

'Wah a—'

'Where.'

'WAAAH a MAH-ther leed her bee-bee.'

'*Laid* her baby.'

'LEED her BEE-BEE.'

I was fighting a losing cause. Not only had Arthur's vowels been carefully cultivated over generations, but his determination to nail my request had unlocked a whole new tone which was best described as a rasping honk. There was no way the poor boy was ever going to be awarded the solo. All I could do now was spare his blushes. As the climactic high note approached, I opened my mouth and sang along.

Moments later, Carolyn returned to the room with my slice of log. 'Wow,' she said. 'How did you get him sounding like that?'

Arthur and I stared at each other.

'You know what?' said Carolyn, placing the cake on top of the piano. 'I think we've got this in the bag.'

Me: Why did I never get to sing the Once In Royal solo when I was young? I could have been the new Aled Jones

Mum: We did ask if you wanted to be a chorister. You said no.

Tuesday, 24 November, Paddington

When I took the 11+ for grammar school entry at my primary school, it was never once suggested I might prepare for the test. One day the teacher simply read out a list of who was down to take it and who was allowed to go and play in the field. One girl who had applied to a comprehensive had no idea why her name was called out until she realised her mum had put down a grammar school as her second choice.

You would struggle to find a parent taking such a blasé approach to the private school admissions process. On the day of the pre-test, both Beatriz and Jocasta kept me keenly updated via text. Despite their sons being in identical situations, the mothers' prose styles differed strikingly. Jocasta went to great lengths to project a sense of calm. She sent brief, present tense updates, forsaking conventional grammar to place me at the heart of the scene. 'Positive vibes,' was her opening missive, not clarifying whether this was an instruction or a report. Another simply said 'On it,' which invited a range of interpretations I felt no need to pin down. The message was clear: everything was going to plan.

Beatriz was not remotely as restrained. I was used to her erratic texting style — she had recently woken me at 6 a.m. by forwarding a video of a cartoon donkey singing 'Silent Night' — but nothing had prepared me for this. 'Today's the day!!!!!' was her indisputable opening gambit. From there, things deteriorated. 'Felix has a headache!!!!!' quickly led to 'He can't concentrate Matt!!!!', followed by 'I don't think he's going to make it!!!!!!!!!!!!!!!!!!!'

I was starting to appreciate Felix's disengaged attitude towards the whole thing. But his mother was heading in the opposite extreme, her anxieties becoming less specific and more ruinous as the day went on. 'Terrified he's blown it!!!?!!' she declared, that stray question mark saying more about her state of mind than any words could. I sent increasingly curt replies until she announced that she was going to get a head massage.

Several hours later, I got a text from Jocasta, who had just picked up Bertie from school.

'All good,' she said.

Zoe: Are you coming to Nikesh's party?
Me: Not this time. I'm not feeling great.

Friday, 4 December, Elephant and Castle

It wasn't a lie. Autumn term had left me exhausted — it didn't seem right that it was only a third of the academic year yet somehow ran all the way from summer to Christmas. I had hoped that entrance test preparation would give me a greater sense of purpose, but all it had done was inflate the anxieties of my clients. The volunteer programme had been postponed until the new year, and my writing itch had started to return. The cinemas were full of Oscar contenders, and I couldn't help notice that none of them were heartwarming comedies. If I was going to write an award-winning script, I needed a more dramatic setting, but I couldn't decide between two options. In the end I doubled my chances and came up with a heart-wrenching drama set in the cut-throat worlds of animal smuggling and gay adoption.

I knew the conventional wisdom was that one cut-throat world was plenty. But I was convinced this was

170

my stroke of genius. As I cycled home from tutoring that day, I was determined to break my writer's block and begin a first draft of the script. When I arrived, there were suitcases in the hallway. I presumed the Frenchman was moving out, and went to bid him *adieu* and confirm the restoration of my personal private bathroom to its rightful custodian. I wasn't surprised he was leaving, since even from the privileged advantage of my self-contained studio flat I had observed that adding a further occupant to the house had brought predictable results. Most pressingly, Bib and her husband had vacated their bedroom for the Frenchman, leaving them and their youngest child to sleep on the living room floor.

The Frenchman was in his room, watching a documentary which appeared from the short clip I saw to be either about climate change or ham. The room was still full of his belongings.

'Moving out?' I said.

'*Non*,' he replied.

Out in the hallway, a Scandinavian woman in a neon sweatband emerged from the kids' bedroom. 'Hey!' she said cheerily. In the living room, Bib was on her hands and knees, setting up four more beds on the floor.

'Oh yeah,' she said. 'Did you meet the new lodgers?'

I turned to see a second Scandinavian woman walking down the hallway carrying a large papier-mâché elephant. 'Hey!' she said, before turning to Bib.

'Which one's our bathroom?'

Me: I have TWO new housemates

Mum: What?! How many of there are you now?

Me: Too many. I need to move out.

Friday, 11 December, Notting Hill

This was meant to be the home where I wrote my Oscar-winning screenplay. Instead I had ended up sharing it with a Frenchman, two Swedish girls, five children and a woman named Bib. There was no need to hang around and find out the Swedish woman's intentions with the papier-mâché elephant. I was about to resort to the indignities of Gumtree when Jocasta asked if I fancied dog-sitting for the weekend.

'Sorry about the mess!' she wrote in a note I found on my arrival. 'Had to pull out all the stops for *Tatler*.'

She didn't understand there wasn't a stray wine glass or dirty plate I couldn't romanticise. Jocasta had said I was welcome to have a friend round, which I took as permission to invite four. Our stated purpose was a reading group, and I am fairly sure someone got out a copy of *Mrs Dalloway* at one point. Three bottles of Sainsbury's prosecco later, we were convinced we were the new Bloomsbury Set.

I had been inside many rich people's homes by this point, but this was the first time I'd had the run of one.

Having so much personal space brings a huge sense of liberation, and I realised that when the cash poor and property rich cling on to their crumbling piles, it is out of more than vanity. The only part I didn't love were my walks with Cromwell the pug, since his unfortunate physiognomy really came into its own when in motion. But every time I thought he was about to gurgle to a permanent halt, he emerged spluttering to fight another day.

When Jocasta got home on Sunday evening, I told her how nice it had been to escape my current living arrangement. I was aware that sharing a three-bedroom flat with ten other people was unsustainable in the long term, but for Jocasta it was beyond the bounds of comprehension.

'You can't stay there, Matt. You should move in here!'

'Here?'

'Sure,' Jocasta said. 'I've been meaning to get a lodger. I won't charge much if you throw in some dog walks and tutoring.'

The offer was quickly shifting from lodger to domestic assistant, but I was far too excited to care. I looked down at Cromwell, who was making his latest attempt to suffocate himself with his own face. I hardly felt thrilled at the prospect of taking him for walks at Jocasta's bidding. But he wasn't the prize. He was the price I had to pay to become part of a household I had been lusting after all term.

'Shouldn't you check with Bertie?'

'Are you kidding? He'll be thrilled.'

Beatriz: Matt! Felix passed the pre-test

Me: That's amazing! Now he can really enjoy his holiday

Beatriz: Actually we were wondering what you're doing next week?

DUBAI

'Look. Do you see? Tallest building in the world.'

I peered out of my taxi window. We were driving along an underpass with high walls on both sides, and all I could see was concrete. If I strained, there was an ugly metallic cylinder peeking over the top in the distance.

'Mmm,' I said.

'Yes,' said Malcolm. 'Wow.'

I had made the mistake of agreeing to share a taxi from the airport with a know-it-all ex-pat. Malcolm worked for a PR company and presumably could afford his own ride, but had pounced on me at the taxi stand. At first I thought he was hitting on me. But it was worse – he wanted to impress me with his knowledge.

'Over there, Jumeirah Beach Hotel. It's in the shape of a wave.'

I could still only see the concrete wall.

'It's next to the Burj Al-Arab. Shaped like a windsail. Get it?'

I got it. It sounded horrific. But again, it was a suspicion I was not able to confirm. Malcolm, however, was captivated by the possibilities that Dubai's demented architectural expansion had afforded.

'Do you know about the world?' he asked. It turned out Malcolm meant The World — an archipelago of 300 artificial islands supposedly built in the shape of the earth's land mass. The way he described it, it sounded like some kind of futuristic theme park. But when I looked it up later, it resembled the baking tray of an eight-year-old who had begun an ambitious shortbread project then got bored halfway through. Africa and South America had been fairly well replicated in cookie-cutter form, but Australia had been inexplicably reimagined as a series of zig-zags.

'And in another part, there will be giant robots walking around.'

Our taxi driver raised an eyebrow.

'Robots?' I said.

Malcolm insisted so, though he was forced to admit that this scheme, along with The World, had been put on hold when the recession hit. Still, not even a global financial crisis could totally thwart the emirate's imaginative vision.

'Here we are,' he said as we pulled up to my hotel. 'Now you will see a whale.'

Malcolm was wrong, but only just. The lobby featured a vast 11-million-litre aquarium containing a four-metre whale *shark*. Hotel guests swarmed and stared in morbid fascination, scarcely able to believe anyone could have had the chutzpah. A Spanish teenager posed for an impromptu *trompe l'oeil* in which the whale shark, hilariously, appeared to be swimming into his mouth. I could only imagine the shark craved the oblivion of a stomach over the glass display case in which it found itself trapped.

I got my key and went up to my room. I had been wanting to stay in a five-star hotel ever since watching the neglected '90s comedy *Dunston Checks In*. It didn't seem right that a cheeky orang-utan had beaten me to it, but the closest I got in my childhood was an overnight stay at a French motorway hotel which wasn't fooling anyone by calling itself 'Première Classe'. As I unpacked in my anonymous suite, I wasn't sure it merited the hype. The fun part about a campsite is how nosy you can be, spying on other families as they empty their potties or pack up their tents. In my family, we liked to give our neighbours nicknames and elaborate back stories. I didn't see how that was going to be possible with all these walls and corridors.

Maybe Dubai was a question of perspective. It was up to you whether you saw a glittering archipelago or a botched cookie experiment, a spectacular ocean scene or a cruel prison. George Northover was not a man ever to pass up a negative reading of a Rorschach test. But if the crash had brought Dubai to its knees, he could restore it to its former glories. The Northovers had come out for a week of winter sun while George negotiated some big money deal involving his hedge. I found him and Beatriz sitting in miserable silence by the pool.

'Did you see the whale?' Beatriz asked.

I wasn't sure if people kept miscategorising the shark because they genuinely didn't realise, or because calling it a whale was the only way to capture the absurdity of what the hotel had done. Either way, you don't correct your client's taxonomy when they are about to pay for your lunch.

'Yes,' I said. 'Wow.'

Felix was retrieved from the nearby waterpark so I could congratulate him on his test success. He gave his usual shrug — there was no reason to get excited about once again having a tutor invade his holiday. I was used to George remaining performatively uninvolved in his son's education. But today he was very concerned by the question of where Felix and I would study.

'I'm not sure they should be working in our hotel room,' George said. 'It doesn't get much afternoon light.'

A survey was launched to determine which room got the most light, but early observations suggested that the sun moved throughout the day, meaning there was no ideal room in which to work.

'What about feng shui?' said Beatriz.

George scowled at her, a reaction Beatriz readily accepted, having not really known herself what she had meant. The exploratory committee began scouting other locations around the hotel, which given its size, turned out to be a considerable task. By the time we had assessed everywhere from the mezzanine lounge bar to what I'm sure was a store cupboard, I was starting to suspect that the exhaustive nature of George's quest had nothing to do with optimum study conditions, only the fact that he didn't have any meetings scheduled that afternoon.

Eventually George found somewhere he liked — a table in a quiet and shady corner. There was only one problem. Someone was already sitting there.

'Sorry,' George said to the older couple seated in the chairs. 'We need these.'

In moments like this, I saw why George was so successful. He knew precisely which words to use to get what he wanted — the exact right amount of explanation, the perfect measure of politeness. For all he knew, the couple were celebrating their golden wedding anniversary, or having their last holiday together before one of them died of a terminal illness. But George hadn't made his fortune by letting himself get distracted by such thoughts. The couple gave each other a confused look, then vacated the seats as George had known they would. Yet still the scene was not quite to his liking.

'Can we move these in a bit?'

George was addressing a passing waiter and pointing at two sturdy mahogany chairs. The waiter was carrying a full tray of plates, but that was no reason in George's mind why he couldn't stop and sort out this infinitely more important matter. A prolonged stare from George was enough to make the waiter put down his tray and drag the chairs closer to the table, upsetting the ergonomics that had been determined at great expense by some Swedish design consultant.

'Great,' George said. 'And let's get rid of this.'

He was pointing at a large crystal vase in the middle of the table.

'The vase?'

'Yes,' George said. 'We don't need it.'

The waiter looked like he was ready to pick up the vase and get rid of George, but bit his tongue and said he would have to speak to his manager. The vase stayed in place for the rest of the week.

In St Moritz, the Northovers had at least had their daily skiing trips to unite them. Out here, George was busy, Felix and Theo obsessed with the nearby waterslide park, and Esme off in Sharm El-Sheikh learning how to scuba dive. Beatriz began bombarding me with texts about potential excursions. I had no desire to be pulled at high speed across the ocean while straddling a giant banana, and couldn't say I was any more keen to be driven into the desert to applaud a belly dancer. The moment riding a camel was proposed, I claimed I had a pressing script deadline, though it was wishful thinking that anyone in the British film industry gave the slightest shit what I was doing that winter.

I had plenty to keep me entertained. My trip had coincided with the Dubai Film Festival, and Peter, the film journalist I had met in Scotland, was attending. Peter was fully accredited at the festival and had got me the hottest ticket in town — a film whose hype had gone into overdrive worldwide. But first he had another assignment.

'Are you sure about this?' I said as we made our way along a hotel corridor. 'Who are we going to say I am?'

'No one. My colleague. It doesn't matter.' said Peter.

Peter already had a youthful appearance, but today was wearing shorts and a bright red backpack which made him look positively adolescent. As we turned up at the media lounge and Peter presented his credentials, the publicity team did a double take, as if he must have won some sort of competition.

'Her Majesty is ready for you,' said the publicist. 'You have ten minutes.'

We were led into a suite to meet the festival's headline guest — Queen Noor of Jordan. She rose as we entered, not to greet us but to present herself in her full glory. She had the same perfectly blow-dried caramel-coloured hair as several of my pupils' mothers, but wore embroidered robes that I'm afraid cannot be described as anything other than regal. As Peter set his dictaphone recording, I was nonplussed about my proximity to royalty, but beside myself to be inside the workings of the film industry. I wasn't entirely sure what role Her Majesty played, but apparently nor was she. She had been invited to deliver the keynote address on the subject of 'Breaking Borders', followed by an appearance on a Cultural Bridge panel. Such titles gave some clue as to the level of cultural intervention we were talking.

'What I want,' Her Majesty said, 'is to use film as a knife to break bread.'

It felt like the kind of metaphor which worked better the less you thought about it, but a perfect moment to whip out one of my tried-and-tested 'Mmms'. Peter let Her Majesty present her talking points, then turned to me.

'Matt, do you have any questions?'

I stared at him. I would need weeks of training before I was capable of making a professional journalistic enquiry. But the evidence before me was that the film industry trotted along happily based on whoever was willing to rock up and talk shit. I took a deep breath.

'Your Majesty — are you looking forward to *Avatar*?'

If anyone exemplified Dubai's fine line between imaginative vision and mad folly, it was James Cameron. That night, the festival rolled out the red carpet for his $300 million blue alien extravaganza. Walking past a bank of photographers was so exciting that I didn't even mind when they lowered their cameras as we approached. Peter and I had got too drunk in my hotel room beforehand for me to remember much of the film. Was there really a scene where the aliens knelt down in a forest and had a group wank?

At the after-party, each table had a glamorous waitress built into the middle of it so that the tablecloths doubled as their skirts. This was a concept which worked better in theory, leaving the waitresses with nothing to do but smile awkwardly as you helped yourself to an hors d'oeuvre. Scanning the room, we noticed a famous Hollywood actor with a certain reputation. As we stared at him, a good-looking younger man sidled up to us.

'You've spotted him then.'

The man revealed that he worked as the actor's assistant. It quickly became clear that his job involved scouring the room for any suggestible young men.

'Do you want to meet him?' the assistant asked with a wink.

As he scurried off to fetch his master, Peter and I hurriedly tried to decide what we would say. I cursed myself for not having completed a draft of my heart-wrenching drama set in the cut-throat worlds of animal smuggling and gay adoption, and wondered if the actor would entertain a verbal pitch.

'Boring,' said Peter. 'Let's ask if he'll fuck us with his Oscars.'

As the assistant brought the actor over, I worried that being prepared to spout bullshit wasn't enough to make it in Hollywood. Maybe I did have to be willing to go all the way. The actor looked us up and down, then moved on without a word. The assistant gave us an apologetic shrug. I turned to Peter.

'Guess we're going to have to make it the hard way.'

Given the ban on serving alcohol, the party wrapped up at a sensible hour. Since sensible was not a word which applied to me or Peter, we went back to my hotel to continue drinking.

'Imagine being gay here,' Peter said. 'What do they *do?*'

Sharing a bottle of airport vodka with a friend in a hotel room was as close as I intended to get to a gathering of homosexuals in a country where sodomy was punishable by death. But as we looked it up online, we learned that the resident gay community took it a few steps further. There was a club night taking place a few blocks down.

'We have to go,' said Peter. 'You only live once.'

'You only die once.'

'It's sodomy that's illegal. They can't arrest us for *being* gay.'

A bottle of vodka later, we found ourselves making our way there. The club was in a hotel basement and was about as lascivious as my Year 6 leavers' disco. Even then, the night had ended with me perching my hands on the hips of a girl called Lauren Barden as we swayed to a contemporary R&B cover of 'Wonderful Tonight'. But here no one was touching, going to great lengths not to risk even grazing the arm of whoever was next to them. At the school disco, we had been carefully monitored by the prudish Mrs Whitfield to make sure boys and girls remained at arm's length. Here it was unclear who was doing the policing.

'I need a cigarette,' Peter said. I couldn't face another red-faced mission through the lobby, so stayed downstairs. I was nervous about being approached, but I quickly noticed I was being viewed with suspicion. We had read online that the scene was rife with undercover cops. It was hard to believe people suspected I might be one, but I realised anyone here might be, and the thought sapped all joy from the occasion. Nights like this were meant to be places where gay people went to be themselves, but this felt like a humiliation, permitting you to identify yourself and nothing more.

Maybe that was something in itself. It was more than I'd dared do with any of my clients. It made no sense, how carefully I kept it hidden compared to the likelihood that it would ever be an issue. What if it was part of a wider concealment dating back to my interview with Philippa and my school years before that? Now that I thought about it, it was impossible to separate the two. I had spent my adolescence obsessing over wearing the right kind of shoes while hiding a deeper secret I was convinced would not be well received. Somewhere along the way, I had internalised the belief that if I was myself, I didn't belong.

Peter came back to the basement shaking. Smoking outside the hotel, he had been approached by the police. His explanations for his presence had not been deemed sufficient, and he'd been thrown into the back of a police car for questioning. At one point he had feared for his life.

My heart raced hearing him recount it. Looking back at the roomful of revellers, I saw their caution in a whole new light. I told Peter they made my problems seem trivial in comparison.

'I'm sure they'd be delighted to hear it,' said Peter.

I blushed, knowing I had only been a few drinks away from pitching a personal essay to *Vice* on how witnessing the oppression of gay men in the Middle East inspired me to return home to London and dry hump classroom assistants with a new sense of pride. Luckily the venue didn't serve alcohol. With a rush of relief, Peter and I joined in the dance.

I woke up with the kind of headache you can expect to get from half a litre of airport vodka. I wasn't due to teach Felix until 4 p.m., which I figured I could manage if I spent the morning having a nervous breakdown in an air-conditioned shopping mall. Then Beatriz texted to ask if I fancied lunch.

'Shall we get a bottle?' she said as I met her at the poolside restaurant. She had secured a table in the sun which was really going to demonstrate the capabilities of her preferred SPF moisturiser. I was fairly sure I was still over the legal driving limit, and hadn't planned on topping myself up with half a bottle of Sauvignon Blanc right before teaching. Before I could think of an excuse, a waiter brought over the bottle Beatriz had already ordered.

'Sorry about all the fuss yesterday,' she said, pouring herself a rare 375ml serving of the Sauvignon. 'George is very particular with Felix. But it's because he has big plans for him.'

As Beatriz elaborated, it transpired that George's big plan was the same one that has served the patriarchy so well over the years — passing the baton to his eldest son regardless of his suitability for the role. I had no idea why George wouldn't want to see his business in the hands of someone sparky and provocative like Esme, but there was no sign this had occurred to Beatriz. Still, she was going to struggle to sell me on notions of paternal inheritance now that I was on my second glass of wine.

'What about you?' I asked. 'Is that what you want?'

As she looked back at me, I got the sense that no one had asked Beatriz about herself in a very long time.

'God, Matt, I don't know sometimes,' she said. 'I really don't.'

Before I knew it, she was telling me her life story. I was hoping to get some dirt on George, or at least a tale about an affair in her youth with a minor celebrity. But the part Beatriz really wanted to tell me, the bit I sensed still kept her awake at night, was that she had begun to train as a lawyer in São Paulo, then abandoned it when she met George and moved to London. There didn't seem to be anything stopping her from resuming training there.

'We don't need me to work,' she said quietly. 'We're very lucky.'

We had got to the end of the wine. Beatriz ordered a pair of margaritas, knowing that even the slightest return to sobriety would make her intolerably self-conscious. I feared I was only one drink away from asking what kept her married to a man like George. But no sooner had the margaritas arrived when he appeared.

'Wine *and* cocktails?' he said, surveying the evidence. 'Aren't you about to teach?'

It was a good point, and one I would have done well to consider sooner.

'Matt only had a sip,' Beatriz claimed improbably. 'He's just off to find Felix, aren't you?'

'Not for another fifteen minutes,' said George, checking his watch.

He took a seat, thrilled at this turn of events. The only thing George preferred to catching someone in the act was having to tease it out of them. 'Sorry I missed out,' he said, examining the empty wine bottle. 'Was it any good?'

As George looked at me, I became aware that I was dripping with sweat. This was hardly a surprise given that I had been happily sitting under the midday sun, but suddenly each droplet felt like an admission of guilt.

'Excuse me,' I said, diving into my bag and pulling out some sun cream. 'I'm feeling the heat.'

George said nothing. He was the type of assassin who waited for his opponent to fall on their sword rather than sticking the knife in himself, so it was important to follow through on my excuse. I tried to squirt some cream into my hand. In my drunken state I squirted out almost the entire bottle.

George glanced down at my handful of cream.

'I burn *really* easily,' I said.

I started applying the cream to my face. Beatriz, sensing I was on a suicide mission, began chattering madly about indoor ski slopes. But George stayed laser-focused on me. I tried rubbing in the cream, but there was so much of the stuff that it formed a protective layer against itself and wouldn't absorb. My circular motion only moved it around my face. I decided a shift in technique was in order, and began to lightly slap my cheeks, hoping against hope it might cause the cream to enter my pores.

'Are you OK?' George said.

'Yes, fine.' And I was. I had come up with a new strategy which involved smearing and pooling the excess cream around the back of my neck. The cream soon reached a critical mass and started to drip down my nape.

'That's better,' I said.

I was sure George had seen right through me. But as long as Beatriz and I stuck together, there was nothing George could do. I glanced at Beatriz. She knew better than anyone that the strength of a lie is not in how convincing it is, but how firmly you are willing to stick to it.

As I walked away from Beatriz and George, I felt what I thought was a wash of relief. Then I realised it was a fresh wave of drunkenness. On top of that, the headache which had initially been numbed by the wine was starting to throb painfully. What if George was the easy part?

'How was Wild Wadi?' I said to Felix once we were seated. I had heard it all before, but the waterslide park was the only thing he ever discussed with any enthusiasm, and I needed some time to pull myself together.

'Oh my god!' Felix said, his eyes lighting up. 'I went on the Super Soaker.'

I urged him to describe it in more detail.

'It's so fast,' he said. 'It's literally vertical.'

That hadn't taken as long as I had hoped.

'Are there any more sort of bendy, windy ones?'

There were. As Felix launched into an involved description of the Mississippi Mud Flow, which I was delighted to learn contained a sharp bend where he had got trapped in his rubber ring for quite a while, I wracked my brains over what I could teach him. The only thing I could bear to consider was creative writing. This would involve Felix doing all the work, with me occasionally leaning in to make sure he'd included a metaphor. All I needed to do was come up with a title.

'The Emu,' I said.

Felix pulled a face. 'The *Emu*?'

I had no idea where I'd plucked that from and regretted it instantly, but if I didn't stick to my guns I might fall apart completely.

'Yes,' I said, as though it was self-explanatory. 'The Emu.'

'What am I meant to write about an emu?' Felix despaired.

'Anything you like,' I said.

It was true. I would accept literally any words he wrote, so long as he sat there and wrote them in silence. I told Felix he could write the humorous diary entry of an emu who has no friends. Or the story of a wealthy man who insists on eating emu at his birthday banquet. Or a criminal nicknamed The Emu. And then I really was done having original thoughts for the day.

Felix refused to write by hand, so I got out my laptop for him to type. As I opened it up, two words screamed out at us: GAY DUBAI. I hadn't touched the laptop since Peter and I researched the nightlife possibilities the previous night. I hurriedly closed the tab, but Felix had seen it. He stared at me.

'Are you gay?'

I had denied it enough times in my life. It wasn't too late for me to tell Felix he'd got the wrong end of the stick.

'Yep,' I said.

'You're kidding.'

He hadn't for a second expected me to admit it. I'm not sure I had either.

'Seriously?' said Felix.

'Seriously.'

Shortly after leaving Dubai, I learned that the whale shark had been freed from the lobby aquarium in response to ongoing protests. The hotel insisted it had been released into the wild. But rumours persisted that it had died in transit.

SPRING TERM 2010

Thursday, 14 January, Notting Hill

'Shall we say £30 a week?' said Jocasta.

'*Thirty?*'

'Great.'

I wasn't sure if Jocasta thought of me as a charity case or was basing the price on a lovely little studio in Marylebone she had rented from her aunt in the eighties. Either way, I suspected her ludicrously favourable room rates didn't extend beyond floppy-haired Cambridge graduates.

'We keep this door open,' said Jocasta, leading me into a part of the house I had never been, 'because Cromwell can get scared and make a mess.'

She was telling me my new home contained a pug who was liable to shit himself, but I could only hear the part about an open door.

'Just in the name of being open,' I said awkwardly. 'I'm gay.'

I had become one of those dreaded homosexuals who, after agonising for years about coming out and finally taking the plunge, gets addicted to the thrill and seeks any opportunity to make another dramatic announcement.

'Matt, I work in fashion. Have you heard of the Big Gay Flash Mob?'

I hadn't. They sounded terrifying.

'It's a club night,' Jocasta clarified. 'Very fashionista but a rollicking good time — and *excellent* men shopping.'

Where had I found this woman? Ten seconds out of the closet and she was trying to hook me up. I felt more confident than ever that this was the start of a beautiful friendship, one which would soon lead to her introducing me to a gorgeous young designer called Florian or Kazimir who could be counted on to give me a good rollicking.

'There's just one rule,' said Jocasta, as if she could see the scene I was envisaging. 'When Bertie's home . . . no fucky fuck.'

Zoe:	NO FUCKY FUCK
Me:	Please. I'm traumatised.
Zoe:	Wait . . . so sucky suck as much as you want?
Me:	Don't
Zoe:	We must know

Saturday, 23 January, Highgate

Beatriz couldn't *believe* I had moved in with Jocasta.

'Gosh, wow,' she said. 'Is she charging you a lot?'

It didn't feel wise to share the generous terms of my arrangement, since there was no knowing what Mumsnet thread it might end up on. Beatriz kept tabs on my progress with Bertie as much as her own son, and there was no doubt she disliked the idea of me moving in with a rival. But Felix kept his cards close to his chest.

'Does Bertie know you're gay?' was all he said.

I wasn't sure, but it had occurred to me that this new spirit of openness was not without its complications. Had Felix told his parents? I didn't like to ask, but the story of him seeing something incriminating on my laptop was one I would rather tell myself or not at all. For now, it was a secondary issue. St Paul's had a mysterious system where candidates who had passed the pre-test were called for a second round of tests one by one at any point between January and June. The school claimed the order was random, but there was fevered speculation that the best candidates were called first. The uncertainty left its young applicants stressed and insecure.

All we could do was keep preparing. The wild card element of this stage was an interview. Officially, it was a way for the schools to get to know the candidates in a more informal setting. In practice, it was the first clue that an education at one of these schools was as much about acquiring social skills as anything you might learn in a classroom. To get Felix in the right mindset I insisted on a full role play, making him stand outside and knock on the door, then shaking his hand and welcoming him in the guise of a friendly housemaster.

'Hello Felix,' I said. 'Welcome to St Paul's.'

Felix gave me a sceptical look. I had already tried this exercise with Bertie, who had slipped effortlessly into the kind of knowing performance mode it required, but Felix was not so theatrically inclined. I pressed on regardless, glancing down the list of question prompts I had found online.

'Right — which scientist or explorer, living or dead, would you most like to meet?'

'Dora.'

'What?'

'The explorer.'

'Come on, Felix. Take this seriously.'

I scanned the list of questions for a safer option.

'Do you have a favourite book or poem?'

'Beans, beans, they make you fart.'

I wanted to offer him a place on the spot. He had twice spotted the absurd potential of the question and held it up for ridicule. The idea that a ten-year-old boy in the twenty-first century might have a favourite poem, rather than be trained to claim that he did, was pure fantasy. In any case, Felix's choice was as valid as any, combining a pulsating rhythm with an offbeat structure. I had always been intrigued by its central claim that the more you fart, the more you eat, since this inversion of the standard cycle of consumption and expulsion hinted at a compulsive narrator who took a depraved pleasure in passing wind. It was the type of literary analysis I would have been happy to conduct had I been in charge of admissions. But we both knew Felix couldn't say this in an interview.

'Fine,' I said, breaking character. 'You choose a question.'

I handed him the list. He scanned it and looked up.

'Do you have any questions you'd like to ask us?'

'What?'

'That's the last question.'

It really was impressive, his ability to troll me like this.

'Oh. Well, do you?'

'Yes.'

Felix pulled a droll expression that would have made Bette Davis proud.

'*What* is the point?'

Zoe: That is genuinely a very good question

Wednesday, 3 February, Notting Hill

The youth volunteer programme was up and running. Martin had taken his time matching mentors with mentees, at one point apologising for 'making this sound like a creepy dating service', which he hadn't until he said that. The first of my charges was Holly, who I had met at bowling and couldn't have been more motivated. Then there was Connor. He was studying at a comprehensive in Leicester and keen to give a talk to his year group. We were meant to have weekly phone calls by dialling in to a conference line with a PIN code, but for several weeks now Connor hadn't shown and I'd been left on hold to Pachelbel's Canon. After a laborious series of manually screened emails, I had finally got him on the line.

'Hey,' he said. 'How are you?'

'I'm good,' I said. 'Just heard the new Lady Gaga single.'

'Oh.'

I was only six years older than Connor. Why was I sounding like some middle-aged music teacher making a doomed attempt to be down with the kids? I always ignored that warning about the call being recorded for training purposes, but if I wasn't careful, Martin would be excerpting clips as a perfect example of what not to do.

'How's your campaign going?' I asked Connor.

'Hmm,' said Connor. 'It still seems to be on pause.'

Connor was meant to be writing a letter to a teacher who hadn't been keen on the idea of him speaking at assembly. I knew I would have crumbled at half as much resistance in Connor's situation. I didn't want to remind him he had been promising to write a draft of the letter for almost a month.

'You just need to write that first draft,' I said. 'Otherwise we're letting the haters get their way.'

In my defence, I *had* just been listening to Lady Gaga. But Connor was going to need more than a half-baked pep talk. The fact that he was on the programme at all was evidence of his investment. Beyond that, I struggled to find the right words.

'Why don't we speak next week, and you can try to do a draft before then?'

'Maybe,' said Connor. 'Can I let you know?'

Saturday, 13 February, Notting Hill

'Don't mind me, Matt,' said Jocasta as she crossed the landing in a translucent kimono. Not being one whose eyes are drawn instinctively to women's nipples, I can't say for sure whether the outfit had a suggestive floral design or betrayed a glimpse of her tumescent areolas. But I have my suspicions.

Jocasta's bedroom was on the floor below, but there was no knowing when she might materialise and in what attire or lack of it. I shared not only a floor but a bathroom with Bertie and his younger sister Isabel. As safeguarding measures go it wasn't exemplary, but I self-monitored to the extent that I couldn't even bear the thought of encountering one of them on my way to the loo in the morning in my T-shirt and boxer shorts. I would edge open my bedroom door and peer through the crack, behaviour far more furtive than anything I was hoping to avoid. It was only when I found myself evaluating the logistics of peeing in a bottle that I hit upon the idea of purchasing a dressing gown.

Isabel was just as fabulous as her older brother. She was six years old and regarded me as a cultural philistine.

'Do you like Justin Bieber?' I asked her over breakfast that morning.

'Why on *earth* would I like him?' she replied with a disdainful bite of granola.

The situation deteriorated as I pretended to know who Laurie Anderson was, and admitted to having seen the remake of *Hairspray* but not the original. I only got back in Isabel's good books thanks to my enthusiasm for hopscotch.

'You're just like another big brother,' she grinned, dragging me out into the garden to play another round.

'Matty!' said Bertie when he found us. 'I've had an idea.'

I wasn't sure if my new diminutive was a sign of his growing affection or an attempt to mark out his territory. But Bertie's idea was one we could all embrace. The other day, I had rather apologetically told him about my cinematic ambitions. Bertie didn't see why we couldn't just make a film ourselves on my phone. He had even conceived a story that put The Don and his ponderous shots of bin men to shame. It centred around a detective named Garbo Folly.

'Is that going to be you?' I asked.

'No no,' said Bertie. 'I'm playing twin sisters accused of murdering each other.'

'Which one's dead?'

'Exactly!'

Isabel declared it unfair that Bertie should get to play both murderer and victim, so Bertie agreed that the twins would murder her instead. All that remained was to cast the titular Garbo Folly. Even my inner attention seeker wasn't convinced I should be denying the lead role to my juvenile co-stars, but something told me attention would be focused elsewhere.

'Shall I wear this?' said Bertie.

He had placed a tea cosy on his head. I couldn't think of any reason why a murderous twin shouldn't don such a costume, and suggested that for Garbo Folly it might constitute an important clue.

'Exactly, Matty!'

It was an interesting choice of refrain, since it was hard to follow the logic of Bertie's creative choices beyond being further showcases for his flamboyance. Maybe there was my answer. As I filmed Bertie skipping across the screen, he did a florid little twirl.

'Oh yes,' Isabel said approvingly. 'Very Pina Bausch.'

Dad:	Pina who?
Me:	She's an iconic choreographer. I can't believe you never taught me.
Mum:	When you were six you were obsessed with Bodger and Badger

201

Tuesday, 16 February, Highgate

The more I embraced life at Jocasta's, the stranger I found it to go to the Northovers. It had taken me a while to understand where they fitted in this country's rigid class hierarchy. They weren't nouveau riche — George was privately educated and Beatriz came from a well-off Brazilian family — but nor were they traditionally upper class. Aristocrats might live in castles, but they tended not to travel by private jet. The sheer size of George's hedge fund meant the Northovers belonged more to a global class defined by their ultra-high net worth. Yet unlike many of their fellow members, they retained a very British belief that it was tacky to spend ostentatiously. Rather than not spend at all — or god forbid, give away their fortune — they lived a life of unimaginable luxury in constant fear of looking like they enjoyed it. No matter how many homes and staff they accumulated, it was empty at its core.

My mission with Felix was starting to feel similarly hollow. The original brief had at least focused on his overall academic prospects. Now we were singularly obsessed with this one goal, and until we knew whether Felix would be following his father to St Paul's, the family's entire future felt on hold.

'It's been a while since I saw you,' said Gustav when I turned up that day.

Since I had switched to teaching Felix at weekends we had stopped crossing paths, but Beatriz had recently added a second weekly lesson.

'Did you miss me?' I said with a grin.

I hadn't planned to flirt, but perhaps the No Fucky Fuck policy was starting to get to me. Apparently Gustav hadn't planned on me flirting either, as we both looked slightly startled and I hurried into the kitchen. I told my friends I didn't have a problem with Jocasta's rule, since it seemed a reasonable compromise for living with one of my pupils. But the jury was out on whether it was a price worth paying.

Felix and Theo were at the breakfast bar, tucking into one of Curtis's enormous spreads. Like everything else in the Northovers' lives, what had first struck me as lavish now appeared totally excessive. Felix was over his dry and crunchy phase, but it was as if the sheer range of what was on offer had left him confused as to what constituted a meal. He was smearing a pain au chocolat with cream cheese, while Theo was following his brother's lead by dunking streaky bacon into some porridge. Theo looked up with a grin.

'Can I make Matt eat this?'

'No,' said Zoraida. 'Go and get dressed. Both of you.'

Actually I was mildly intrigued by the bacon porridge, but I could see Zoraida was in need of a reprieve. I guessed she would be all fired up for one of our bitching sessions, but as soon as Felix was out of earshot she looked at me with concern.

'I'm worried about him, Mateo,' she said. 'He's not himself.'

The longer term had gone on, the worse Felix's mood had got. Some of his classmates had begun to get called for interview, but the Northovers had heard nothing. Unsurprisingly, Felix hadn't said a word, but if Zoraida had noticed too, it was clear the pressure was getting to him. I told Zoraida I'd try speaking to him, admitting he had opened up in the past. But once we were alone, he was less forthcoming than ever. All he would say was that he didn't care.

'You *can* tell me how you feel,' I said. 'I won't tell anyone.'

'I need the loo.'

'Seriously, Felix?'

'Cream cheese. Makes me shit.'

Beatriz: Hi Matt. Can I give you a call?

Wednesday, 24 February, Notting Hill

For once, I was happy to hear from Beatriz. I hadn't dared raise my concerns with her, but presumably Zoraida had passed them on, and I was relieved Beatriz thought it worthy of a chat.

'Thanks for calling,' I said in my most concerned voice.

'I'm just confused,' said Beatriz. 'What does it mean?'

I hesitated for a second.

'Felix is *ahead* of Bertie in the alphabet,' Beatriz despaired.

How had I let myself think she might actually be worried about her son's mental state? Something far worse had happened — Bertie had been invited to interview first.

'Apparently it's random,' I said hopefully.

'No one believes that,' Beatriz snapped.

Nothing I said would convince her otherwise. All I could do was placate her until she got tired and hung up. I attempted to meet her halfway by suggesting that this news might be tough for Felix to hear. But Felix's state of mind wasn't on Beatriz's list of concerns.

'Have you done anything differently with Bertie?' she asked.

I wouldn't put it quite like that. I had barely done much at all. Bertie was better at applying himself than Felix, but Jocasta's big advantage over Beatriz was that she cared less. In retrospect, our meeting at Electric House had been more about assessing my personality. It was an attitude that was beyond Beatriz.

That evening, Jocasta came to inform me about her latest trip to Paris.

'Great news about the interview,' I said without thinking.

Jocasta gave me a look. Bertie was at his dad's, so it was obvious who my source was. But Jocasta wasn't going to lower herself to Beatriz's level.

'Yes,' she said. 'Great news.'

Me: I've got the house to myself this weekend
Zoe: OMG I'm there

Saturday, 6 March, Notting Hill

'It's so depressing,' I said to Zoe. 'I'm not teaching them anything.'

'God no,' said Zoe. 'You're getting them on the guest list at Annabel's.'

We were sitting in Jocasta's living room, following in a long bourgeois tradition of critiquing society while drinking tea from fancy china. Jocasta didn't mind how often I had friends round, unless of course they were friends with benefits. It was hard to find many positives about the entrance test process, but it wasn't all bad. I showed Zoe the film I had made with Bertie.

'Oh my god, this kid is a star!'

'I know. Good job he's ten years younger than me.'

Zoe pulled a face and asked what I meant. I told her I'd never encountered children with this level of cultural awareness — they were exactly the kind of people who would be at the front of the line if they ever wanted a career in the arts.

'I'm sure there are people who say that about you. You're not exactly Oliver Twist.'

'I am compared to these kids.'

'Matt, come on — there are always going to be people more privileged than you somewhere. So many people would kill to be in your position. Look where you're living!'

She was right and she knew it.

'I'll tell you the one thing these kids have over you,' said Zoe. 'It's a mindset. You can call it entitlement if you want, but . . . why don't *you* make a short film?'

The first time this had been suggested, I had recoiled. But there was no denying how much fun I'd had with Bertie and Isabel. It reminded me of the plays I'd put on as a child, a habit that had followed me throughout school and university. But somewhere in recent months, it had run aground. Whatever was going to reignite that spark, I was fairly sure it wasn't a heart-wrenching drama set in the cut-throat worlds of animal smuggling and gay adoption. Maybe a short film was not a diminishment but a stepping stone.

'I'd love to,' I said to Zoe. 'But I don't have a budget. I don't have anything.'

'You'll figure that out. There are no rules. Just make *something*.'

Me: New plan. I'm going to be a director.
Mum: Good idea. Have you watched *Wallander*?

Thursday, 11 March, Waterloo

Connor had dropped out of the volunteer programme. Martin put a positive spin on it, but it was hard to avoid the feeling that I was a flop. My reputation was salvaged by Holly. She had been dialling in to our weekly phone calls at the appointed hour without fail, but that week the conference line was down. Martin suggested I come into the office to make my call.

'Hey!' said Holly as we were connected. 'Let me fill you in.'

Holly was on top of everything. She had negotiated a series of eight workshops for her college year group and planned them in impeccable detail. The first one was taking place next week.

'How are you feeling?' I asked.

'Fine.'

'Try not to care too much what people think.'

'I won't.'

'Just be true to yourself.'

'Yeah,' said Holly. 'I'm not worried. To be honest, I'm already thinking about what I can do next.'

As she told me her plan, I listened in admiration. When I signed up to be a youth mentor, I had envisaged the sort of inspirational moments and unearned breakthroughs you'd find on a mid-season episode of *Glee*. But just as with tutoring, it was much more common to feel surplus to requirements, for better or worse. Afterwards, I found Martin and told him I didn't think I had much to offer Holly.

'She's impressive,' he admitted. 'But don't underestimate what she gets from you.'

'I'm just saying "Great" a lot.'

'Perfect,' said Martin. 'You might be the only person who is.'

Thursday, 18 March, Notting Hill

'Matty darling!' said Bertie. 'Good news.'

As always with Bertie, it was impossible to know whether he was being himself or performing a character. But there was no questioning the news. Despite never doubting that Bertie would be awarded a place, Jocasta was delighted and took the rare step of inviting her ex-husband Giles in for a drink. He was trim and well dressed, with the kind of middle-aged good looks that convince a certain type of man it is time to leave his wife for a twenty-seven-year-old. I knew instantly that we had nothing in common, and was delighted our encounter would be limited to a polite glass of champagne. But Bertie had other ideas.

'Can we show Dad the film we made?'

'Ah yes,' said Giles, eyeing me with suspicion. 'I forgot you're Mr Spielberg.'

I could see why Jocasta had divorced him. I had no desire for this man to sneer over my performance as Garbo Folly. But as the film began to play, I realised the person most concerned about Giles's reaction was Bertie. While his twin alter egos pranced about on screen, I thought of the day aged eighteen when I got an offer from Cambridge, then came out to my parents that evening. In retrospect, I chose a day when I presumed myself high in their estimations because I was scared — needlessly, it turned out — that my other news would not clear such a bar. Bertie appeared to have made a similar calculation.

'Hilarious!' said Jocasta, who was watching for at least the fourth time.

'Yes,' said Giles tightly. 'Very fun.'

Bertie's face fell. He needed more than that. I suddenly felt like I knew why Jocasta had wanted to meet prospective tutors. She worried about Bertie, and how the world would receive her son. God knows what I had said or done that day in Electric House to convince Jocasta that Bertie and I were so well suited. But right now, I knew what he needed. It might seem unlikely that all it took was a look, especially one that on the surface amounted to little more than that mildly benevolent puckering of the dimples you give someone who has just passed you the divider at a supermarket checkout. But behind my eyes was a kinship only visible to someone who has felt that same stirring of difference, that aching need for acceptance, within themselves. Bertie's place at St Paul's hadn't taken an ounce of effort. But as he looked back in gratitude, I realised his parents had got their money's worth.

SPRING TERM 2010

Sunday, 21 March, Notting Hill

'Hello Matt,' the woman said. 'I heard you got Bertie into St Paul's.'

It was terrifying how fast word spread in this world. Did the yummy mummies have a spreadsheet? Bertie had only heard the news a few days ago, but already someone had got hold of my number. She introduced herself as Claudia, then identified as a friend of Beatriz. It was perhaps no surprise that it was Beatriz and not Jocasta who couldn't shut up about Bertie's achievement. People loved to attribute it to me directly, as though I had personally smuggled Bertie into St Paul's under cover of night. I told Claudia that considering Bertie's intelligence, it had not been a huge challenge.

'Not for you, I'm sure.'

I was embarrassed for her. She was acting like I was some legendary witch doctor she had finally tracked down after a month-long trek, and was now having to flatter for my custom. If she had stopped and thought about it, her evidence of my talent was virtually nil. But the hysteria at the London prep school gate had convinced Claudia I had magical powers.

'So are you available to tutor Leo?' Claudia asked.

I hesitated. I needed some work for next term, but every aspect of the admissions process made me want to get away from it as soon as I could.

'I'm not sure I have any slots,' I said.

'You must be able to squeeze us in. We're happy to pay what it takes.'

It was crazy how invested people were. Maybe Claudia was playing the long game and knew that paying over the odds was a shrewd investment in a project that would ultimately end with her son securing a Cabinet position. The question was not how much she was willing to pay, but how much I could bring myself to ask for.

'So is he applying next year?' I asked Claudia.

'Oh no, not for a while yet,' said Claudia. 'He's just turned seven.'

Mum:	Have you decided when you're coming home for Easter?
Me:	Sort of. I'll call you.

TUSCANY

'It's torture, Matt,' Beatriz declared. 'Absolute torture.'

As she lay back on her sun lounger and sipped her cocktail, I wondered if I ought to inform Amnesty International.

'It's because they come from everywhere nowadays!'

It was an astonishing comment from someone who was herself an immigrant, but Beatriz was right that it was the international demand for English private school places that had driven the competition to such heights. If only she knew I'd been working for the Russians.

Because the Northovers couldn't focus on anything else until this was resolved, I had been invited to join them for a week at their villa in Tuscany. I had been looking forward to going home to Dorset for Easter, but when I mentioned the clash to Beatriz, she offered to fly me business class. It was impossible to say no. My income had been stable for a while now, but I was still conscious of the cost of everything in my daily life, constantly evaluating whether or not my purchases had been worth it. As I boarded my flight and accepted a complimentary glass of champagne, I took a photo to send my parents, then decided against it.

The villa was a spectacular hilltop property approached by a long, tree-lined drive. An infinity pool looked out over vineyards, while the garden hummed with cicadas and was invariably drenched in golden sunlight. The scene was only spoiled by Beatriz's relentless anxieties and George's determination not to appease them. Instead he wandered around finding flaws in the villa and things that Gustav ought to have dealt with before our arrival. I was starting to understand why George was so incapable of relaxing and enjoying his life. When you've invested your hard-earned cash in something, you feel a kind of determination to enjoy it. If money is no object, it's a lot easier to wonder what the point is.

'Good news,' said Beatriz, looking up from her phone. 'I've just removed a rather overbearing friend and mother from Felix's social life.'

Removed? By what method? Had she ordered a hit on them?

'I think next term we'll cut down on play dates generally,' Beatriz said. 'And have you come three times a week.'

'I'm happy to do whatever you and George think is best.'

'She's the boss,' said George without looking up.

All signs suggested that this was going to be a difficult week. But failing to appreciate a place like this made me as bad as them. Across the garden, Theo was bouncing on a trampoline with the daughter of the villa's Albanian housekeeper, who was about the same age as him. They got on like a house on fire, communicating in a made-up language that borrowed freely from English, Italian and Albanian as required. It was charming to observe, but I couldn't help thinking it was the kind of bond that would become unspokenly *verboten* in a year or two. Give it thirty, and the girl would be cleaning up after Theo while he ignored his wife and fretted about the size of his annual bonus. I watched the two of them jump up and down and wondered if Beatriz ever had similar thoughts.

'Percy Langbourne,' Beatriz said. 'That's another boy we need to remove.'

Esme had joined us on the trip, but was singularly consumed by her task for the holiday — conceiving an idea for her art A-Level exam piece. I was amazed that Beatriz and George weren't able to see the cautionary tale their daughter presented. By whatever method it had taken, Esme had made it by the skin of her teeth into the same kind of top tier school where Felix was applying. But that was the start of her problems. Few things can be more demoralising than being constantly bottom of the class among a group of high achievers. I could see how stressed her art project was making her, but apparently so could Beatriz. A few days in, she asked if I could help stimulate some ideas.

'What kind of art are you into?' I asked Esme.

'I'm not really,' Esme lamented.

This was a shame for someone who was taking the subject at A-Level. Luckily we were staying in a property which contained an original Giacometti and several impressive examples of the Flemish school. I walked Esme through our personal private gallery, but none of it sparked her interest.

'I'm thinking more like Damien Hirst?'

Not him again. I asked what it was she liked about his art, hoping it wasn't those fucking dots. Esme was limited to a vague memory of his formaldehyde shark, but I pushed her to connect it to some related image or theme.

'Fish?'

It was a start. Soon Esme was talking angrily about pollution and wondering if it would be possible to construct a fish from plastic bags.

'What about a plaster cast?'

I'd made one for my own GCSE project, and it was the only art skill I knew. Esme loved the idea and Beatriz was thrilled to see her finally enthused. Before I knew it, Esme and I were in a car to Siena to purchase the necessary supplies.

'Let's get like a massive tuna,' Esme said. 'They're really endangered.'

Her commitment to the cause was to be applauded, but given that tuna could grow up to four metres in length, it felt wise to impose some parameters. I suggested she scale down her idea, at least to start with. We arrived at the fishmonger and Esme approached the counter.

'Hi, I'd like a large fish, please . . . but just the face.'

The fishmonger rolled his eyes in a way which suggested this wasn't the first idiotic request he'd handled from a tourist, maybe even that day.

'Just the *face*? Are you sure?'

'Yeah,' Esme said. 'To start with.'

The fishmonger crossed muttering to his assistant, but Esme was buzzing. She turned to me with a grin.

'Watch out, Damien Hirst.'

Despite the distractions his siblings provided, there was no avoiding the purpose of my trip. I felt Felix and I had done as much preparation as we possibly could, but the only comfort Beatriz drew from our protracted wait was that it gave us more time. She insisted we work for four hours a day. I tried to make her see that this was insane, but it was hard without sounding like I was trying to do less work myself. Instead I declared that we would do two hours before lunch and two after, with a ten minute break every hour on the hour, apart from lunch, which would last an hour.

'So, seventy minutes,' said Felix.

'No.'

I knew maths was a weak spot, but this was concerning.

'Yeah, cos I get a ten minute break every hour. Lunch break, plus ten minutes.'

I wished he showed this much imagination when it came to his studies, but you could hardly blame him. In the end it was a moot point, since it was impossible to get Felix to start on time. Two days into our regime, I was walking over from my room when he sent me a text. 'I'm still asleep,' was his miraculous claim. I told him I was almost there.

'Go back to your room,' came his response.

The next day I was already waiting for him at our desk when he texted.

'I'm gonna take a shit.'

'Can't it wait?'

'I am wiping my bum.'

Something didn't add up, but I wasn't about to text a ten-year-old about his bum. I was happy to lose a few battles, since getting Felix to lessons was the easy part.

'Righty-ho,' I said in the guise of a posh Dickensian schoolmaster. 'Shall we peruse some algebra?'

'Jesus,' said Felix.

I had got so bored with revising the same material that I had turned to my mum for tips. She had recommended comedy accents as a good way to liven up a revision session, a suggestion that had not required a hard sell on someone who needed little excuse to turn an everyday situation into a stage. Cornelius Hazelwood — naturally I gave him a name — saw to it that Felix could tell his prime numbers from his square roots. Then Beryl Swinehodge, an imperious Yorkshire matriarch, rolled up to test him on food pyramids. The less said the better about Dieter von

Peter von Düsseldorf, an allegedly German *Kappelmeister* and part-time drill sergeant who reinvented the water cycle as a light operetta. While I managed to elicit the odd chuckle from Felix, it was a struggle even for this all-star staff room. At the end of one day, Felix had had enough. He collapsed his head onto the table.

'Just want to stop breathing,' he murmured.

I was pretty sure he wasn't serious, but it was still alarming.

'If you do that, you'll die.'

'Good.'

Whenever the Northovers left the villa, I was ecstatic. I wasn't strictly alone, since the homes of the super-rich are never devoid of staff. I was on friendly terms with the various cooks and cleaners and gardeners who populated the property, but I had stopped trying to pretend I was one of them. That didn't mean I was capable of relaxing in their presence. I would gaze at the pool and imagine myself leaning on the edge with a cocktail like some mysterious house guest in a Bertolucci film. But no sooner had I made myself a drink and got in position than I felt embarrassed, and wondered how long I had to leave it before getting out.

'That looks nice,' said a familiar voice.

Blushing, I turned to see Gustav.

'What are you doing here?' I said without thinking. He hadn't been in St Moritz or Dubai, so I'd assumed that a butler didn't travel with the family.

'I've come to sort out a few things for George.'

The slightest of raised eyebrows was the closest I would ever get to him bitching. It was a curious role, the butler. There was little wonder it had proved such an enduring character in plays and murder mysteries over the years. I couldn't imagine the Northovers being shocked or even annoyed to learn that Zoraida complained about them all the time, but Gustav was defined by his loyalty. Where was the rage? Working in servitude for a man like George, never allowing your temper to flare . . . it had to be buried somewhere. Maybe Gustav got pissed with his mates and called George a twat, but he acted like he'd take a bullet for him. Knowing I would never penetrate this façade only added to his allure.

I tended to eat with the family, but it was as if Gustav had an invisible feeding tube, as I couldn't figure out when or how he fed himself. He might have forever remained to me a person without thoughts and desires and bodily functions if it hadn't been for his exercise routine. Gustav was staying next to me in the converted stables. On my lunch break the next day, I went to my room to lounge on my bed in the shade. In front of my window was a yard area not visible from the main property. By pure coincidence I am sure, Gustav appeared there in a little vest and shorts and began working out. At first I was embarrassed, and grabbed a back issue of *Vogue Italia* that had been left on a side table, learning more about the private passions of Monica Bellucci than I ever thought I would. But it soon became obvious that Gustav was putting on a show.

The most reliable barometer of this was the grunting. To start with, Gustav executed his crunches and press ups in silence, but soon he was making muffled exclamations of the sort one makes during pleasurable but not entirely effort-free sex. Next, he started producing the kind of mezzo forte moans I would reserve for a bed partner who requires almost constant reassurance. I am not going to embarrass him by claiming that by the end of the routine he was groaning like a mating walrus, but his audio commentary headed in a direction both suggestive and impossible to miss.

How to respond? In the animal kingdom, I would have offered some equivalent or complementary mating call, but that felt neither appropriate nor erotic. I adopted a more passive role — not like that, don't get ahead of yourself — and increased the amount of eye contact. At first I was coy, glancing up from beneath heavy eyelids in what I presumed was the manner of a bashful Hollywood starlet. But after checking in the mirror, it appeared it was closer to someone having an epileptic fit. This was not an arena in which subtlety would be rewarded. The next day when Gustav repeated his routine, I stared openly at him until he met my gaze and held it.

That night, I woke to find Gustav on top of me, sweaty and smelling of beer.

'Oh,' I said. It was a polite response to someone who has entered your room in the middle of the night and straddled you, but I was relieved I hadn't panicked and gone with 'How do you do?' This wasn't Gustav but a secret, midnight version of him. I never would have pegged him as a beer drinker, but I had only ever seen his professional side. Now that I had got my hands on the real Gustav, I wondered if I preferred the fantasy version. But I decided to embrace the experience. I knew he would be zipped back up into his immaculately pressed clothes before dawn.

Gustav left the next morning. Far from distracting me in my lessons, his presence had put a spring in my step. Now he was gone, I hit a wall. Much as I suspected Felix had been being melodramatic when he claimed he wanted to stop breathing, I didn't want to take any risks. Instead of doing any more revision, I suggested we embark on a writing project of Felix's choosing. I didn't expect much based on his creative writing history, but to my surprise he was up for it. He gave his story the original title of 'Fighting Club'. It was about a young man who wins his spurs in a gladiatorial arena where fights are staged between, for example, an armoured tiger and a flame-throwing elephant. The protagonist's name was Matt.

'Nice,' I said.

It might seem odd that having an eleven-year-old name his main character after me in a holiday *Bildungsroman* could be so touching, but I took it as confirmation of the esteem in which Felix held me. The character was a shrewd invention on Felix's part, since there was no way I could meet his expectations in real life. It would be 'Matt' who lived out his fantasies of strength and heroism, and for that he needed a mutant pal with the body of a camel and the head of a duck.

'Wait,' I said — and I was ready to pause production on the first edition print run if we didn't get this right — 'do you honestly think that thing is going to be able to beat a flame-throwing elephant?'

'Matt will train him,' Felix assured me.

'Fighting Club' just about got me to the end of the week. By the time we reached our penultimate morning, I was dreaming of sitting in bed at home with a microwave curry and an illegal download of *Gilmore Girls*. But first I had to get through one last evening.

'I'm not sure about San Giuseppe,' said George. 'We didn't like their trout.'

'It was fine,' said Beatriz. 'Maybe slightly subpar.'

A slightly subpar trout was more than enough reason for George to throw their carefully organised plans into chaos. Beatriz began listing possible alternatives, but none of them satisfied George.

'What about Il Campo?'

'Lovely,' said Beatriz. 'If Gustav can manage that.'

As George headed inside, I turned to Beatriz.

'Is it hard to get a table there or something?'

'Not exactly,' said Beatriz. 'It's just . . . in Rome.'

You'd be amazed how little hassle it is to go to Rome for supper when someone else is handling arrangements and going to every possible effort to make it smooth. Later that day, around 6 p.m., a car took us to a nearby helipad, from where it was a mere forty-five minutes to our destination. No one spoke for the entire ride, with not even George unable to appreciate the thrill of gliding over the Tuscan hills. As we landed in Rome and a second car drove us to the restaurant's entrance, I imagined Beatriz in some alternate life in suburban Milton Keynes, insisting to a friend that it wasn't too much trouble to take the kids to Chessington World of Adventures. 'Honestly, it's really quite convenient. Ninety minutes, door to door.'

The restaurant was Michelin-starred and perched on a hill overlooking the city, in case the clientele needed any reminder of their status. Even a year earlier, the thought of visiting somewhere like this would have resulted in me laying out several outfits and agonising over the appropriate level of dressiness. But I had figured out that the best way to fit in around people with money was to project a constant attitude of not giving a shit. As we entered, I spotted several tables that looked more fun than our party — glamorous fashion types or extravagant sugar daddies. I watched George scowl at the various ways our fellow diners had degraded themselves by dressing up too much for the occasion, going overboard on the plastic surgery or otherwise suggesting that being rich might actually be quite fun.

'We came here by helicopter!' I wanted to scream.

I looked at the menu and picked out a dish which sounded nice without being excessively indulgent for the Northovers' tastes.

'So what were you revising today?' George asked once the waiter had taken our orders.

I froze and looked at Felix. Lessons had deteriorated so much on our final day that we had given up on Fighting Club in favour of a passionate debate over whether we would rather have a metre-long neck or a beak instead of a mouth.

'The Battle of Hastings,' I said.

It was a pretty safe bet. We had gone over it earlier in the week and Felix knew it backwards.

'Excellent,' said George, turning to Felix. 'Who won?'

The only confusing part about the Norman Conquest is that there were two Harolds, but one was conveniently slain before he ever got to Hastings. It actually helped in remembering that both Harolds were losers in the end.

'You know this one,' I said to Felix. 'Was it Harold or William?'

I was prepared to flout whatever rules would let us claim a victory. I wanted to take back everything I'd once said to Felix about pausing before you answer. He knew it was William. His name was William the *Conqueror*, for god's sake. But the pressure was preventing Felix from connecting the right synapses.

'Harold,' Felix said.

George was the kind of person who comes alive when disaster strikes. Here, in the form of a single wrong answer, was evidence that things were bad, very bad, worse than even he had dared to dream. As the waiter brought our starters, George was foaming with disappointment.

'Come on then,' George said. 'Is he unteachable?'

It was an extraordinary question to ask of any child, let alone your own, in their presence. It was the kind of last-ditch query I imagined being made about a boy who had been expelled from multiple schools, not one who'd muddled up the winners and losers of 1066.

'I wouldn't say *that*,' I started. But was I sure? A part of me did fear that Felix's wrong answer was symptomatic of a wider malaise, and that it was already too late to inspire in him any genuine desire to learn.

'So what have we been paying you for?' said George.

He was incapable of seeing this as anything other than a failed return on his investment.

'Let's not blame Matt,' said Beatriz. 'Felix hasn't failed yet.'

'He'd better not,' snarled George. 'Otherwise this has all been a big waste of time and money.'

SUMMER TERM 2010

Me: Hey Conrad – this is Matt, Jocasta's lodger.
              She suggested I get in touch to talk about
              filmmaking.
Conrad: Nice one. I'll give you a call!

Saturday, 17 April, Shepherd's Bush

The thing about nepotism is that it's completely inconceivable to those who don't have access to it, and the most natural thing in the world to those who do. As soon as I told Jocasta about my plans to make a film, she hooked me up with her godson, a budding producer. After my experience with The Don, I was wary of grifters. But Conrad not only sounded serious, he had a short film going into production and some spaces on his crew, if I was interested. He asked me to meet him at his studio in West London.

I had decided that if Conrad and I got on, I would ask him to produce my short film. The fact that I hadn't written it yet was a minor issue. Conrad's studio was on a smart residential street, and felt as if someone had won the lottery then spent it all on converting a garage. From the moment I walked in, I got a rush of excitement. There were a dozen people hard at work, poring over scale models of sets or making detailed notes about costumes. Conrad was only a few years older than me but felt like a professional, a judgement I am admittedly basing on the fact that he was wearing a polo neck and holding a clipboard.

'We could really use a script supervisor,' he said. 'Have you done that before?'

'Yes,' I said.

I was more than happy to lie about my experience, though as I said it I remembered that I had once served as line prompt during a rehearsal for a junior school production of *The Lion, The Witch and The Wardrobe*. Conrad had sent me the script for his short film in advance — a modern fairy tale called 'Ali and the Lamp' which was full of wacky special effects. He explained that the simpler method would be to rely on VFX that could be done in post-production, or 'fixed in post' as he called it. But his plan was to use vintage trickery which could be captured on camera. 'Fair warning,' said Conrad, 'we're going to be working with an actual pig.'

The following week, I turned up on set. There were even more people than I'd seen at the studio, all appearing to know their function precisely. I thought about saying hello, but it was a risk when I still only had the most rudimentary grasp of what it meant to supervise a script. Besides, the only crew member I cared about meeting was the pig.

First on our schedule was a scene set in a Lebanese restaurant on Edgware Road. The call sheet listed Ali, Genie and PIG. I checked my script, making sure I knew the exact moment that PIG appeared. An animal handler arrived on set and I met the artiste who would be interpreting the role of PIG. Sure enough, it was an actual pig. Actually it was a piglet, though I wasn't sure if that had always been the plan or it had beaten several actual pigs to the role.

'Quiet on set, guys,' said Conrad. 'We don't want to upset the pig.'

The pig was the least of our problems. Conrad had failed to consider the fact that filming with an actual pig in a Muslim restaurant might not be the best idea. We were halfway through PIG's big scene when a crowd of locals began to form. At first, they were only curious. But when they saw what was happening, the objections began. Before long, the crowd was getting angry and there was trouble in the air.

'Fuck,' said Conrad. 'We're gonna have to jump ship.'

It was a wise decision, even if I was starting to suspect that Conrad's professionalism equated to little more than The Don's bravado with better scheduling and a few more resources. Either way, in my role as script supervisor I was duty bound to inform him that we had not got all the shots we needed of PIG.

'It's fine,' said Conrad, 'we'll fix it in post.'

Matt: I'm not sure he's the producer for me
Zoe: What are you talking about? That is exactly
           the kind of man who wins Oscars

Monday, 26 April, Mayfair

I had turned down the woman who wanted me to prepare her seven-year-old for an 11+ entrance exam. The thought of giving a child that age even the vaguest dose of admissions anxiety four years in advance was too much to stomach. Rather than take a risk on a new client, I decided to return to the familiar terrain of the holding pen. Unlike any other job, you could dip in and out depending on your availability. This didn't strike me as any less mad than it always had done, but it was an approach that happened to suit me that term.

The hallway felt different, but I guessed it was an illusion. Then I realised it was the smell. It was a perfume — a subtle, floral one, the kind that was only offered by the sales assistants at Harrods once they had got a good look at your shoes and decided you were the kind of woman who could afford it, and would then explain its grace notes of pine and jojoba with all the rapture of someone who worked on minimum wage for commission. Did it belong to the boys' mother?

Surely. It wasn't Nadia, and it didn't strike me as the kind of thing a tutor would wear. But before I could trace it to its source, Nadia had assigned me Emil and sent me upstairs.

Emil was now six and far more well behaved than the boy who had asked me to swish his bottom. If he recognised me at all, he didn't let on. I asked him a few friendly questions about the computer game he was playing, but Emil had long ago learned that striking up a rapport with a tutor was a waste of his time.

'Right, where's your homework folder?'

'Downstairs.'

'Do you want me to go and get it?'

I wasn't trying to be helpful. I wanted to follow the scent and see where it led. It felt too late to ask Nadia where the boys' parents were, but I couldn't believe I had ever been happy to teach them without knowing the answer.

'No,' said Emil.

He led me downstairs to retrieve the folder. As we entered the study, I saw his bag in the corner, but Emil crossed over to a desk and pulled open a drawer as if he might find it there. The drawer was filled with rolls of £50 notes. It had to amount to tens of thousands of pounds, if not more. Emil did an unsubtle glance over his shoulder then shut the drawer. He pretended to spot his bag and we headed back upstairs. But I had seen what he wanted me to see.

Me: If I go silent, inform the police
Zoe: ???

Monday, 10 May, Highgate

I had been dreading my first visit to the Northovers since Tuscany. I couldn't decide if I was more worried about bumping into Gustav or catching the end of George's temper again. Maybe David Cameron's election would have put George in a good mood, since even with my limited knowledge I could only assume that a Conservative government was good news for hedge funds. But as I arrived, I heard shouts coming from George's study.

'If my door is open and you see a dirty teacup — quick, quick, quick!'

Moments later, Zoraida came striding into the kitchen. '*¡Este hombre!*'

I wasn't sure if she had faith in George's lack of Spanish or was past the point of caring. But this was about more than a dirty cup.

'He won't let me see my brother,' Zoraida despaired.

She explained that her brother had fallen seriously ill in Colombia and she wanted to go and visit. Since she was unable to give a definite date for her return, George had suggested that her position with the family was similarly up in the air.

232

'That's outrageous,' I said. 'They could afford it if you're gone a year.'

'*Por favor*, Mateo — it's not about the money.'

George felt at liberty to take out his frustrations on anyone in his path, but it was no coincidence that the blows landed most frequently on his staff. Nor was it hard to compute why I got an easier ride than Zoraida. For years, she had swallowed the indignity. Now George held her fate in his hands.

'Ay Mateo. I promised myself when I came here — *no voy a limpiar pisos.*'

I'm not going to clean floors. In Colombia, Zoraida had been a university secretary and had never imagined when she moved to London that she would end up doing domestic labour. She wasn't being a snob. But she knew what it meant to be an immigrant and spend your days being treated as less than human.

'Do you want this?' she asked.

It was the £40 jar of artichokes we had originally bonded over.

'I'm not hungry.'

'Take it! They're never going to eat them.'

'Not now they're not!'

I squirrelled the jar into my backpack. If it made Zoraida feel better even for a moment, I was all for it. But we both knew it was a sad excuse for a victory.

Zoe: Bastard

Friday, 14 May, Notting Hill

I wasn't sure how I felt about living at Jocasta's now that I was no longer teaching Bertie. It was hard to imagine a more beautiful place to live for so little rent, but was that really why I had been drawn to living there? Jocasta might have given me access to a rarefied world, but my experience with Conrad and PIG had taught me that I needed to be taking risks and making mistakes among people my own age. Besides, I had realised Jocasta was far from the influential fashionista she first appeared. She belonged to a side industry for people who had a lot of time to attend parties. Never had this been more apparent than tonight, when she was hosting a soirée. It was one of those words I didn't expect anyone to say with a straight face. It was what you called an event that was neither fun enough to be a party nor accomplished enough to be a concert. Maybe this would be the soirée to change my mind.

My prejudice was given credence almost immediately by the revelation that there was to be a live performance by some snails. An artist arrived that afternoon to set up the act, which involved vertical strips of sandpaper on which the snails were placed so they could inch up and down. I am sorry to report that this was accompanied by a saxophonist. That evening, as guests arrived, they marvelled vocally at the snails and the saxophone and what it all meant. This was an infinitely more fascinating performance.

Where was Virginia Woolf when you needed her? At this point I'd settle for Leonard Woolf. I was stuffing my face with canapés and debating the risks of doing a withering Facebook post about the snails when a miserable-looking American man in a velvet suit sidled up to me. He was one of those people who had a sad story and was going to tell it to you — not once you got to know him, but imminently. 'Hello,' he said simperingly.

My heart sank. He was interested in me, but it was an interest I could never satisfy. While he may have thought he wanted to get in my pants, he would only ever find peace by murdering his father or excavating his trauma in a clinical setting. But here we were in front of the vol-au-vents, so I asked how he knew Jocasta.

'It's a funny story actually,' he said with an incredibly mirthless expression. I helped myself to another vol-au-vent, knowing I was going to need all the energy I could get in order to summon a laugh. But then he started asking me questions. I had no interest in providing him with any personal information, but even at a cursory mention of my short film plan, his eyes lit up.

'How interesting,' he said. 'I happen to be a big supporter of the arts.'

Nadia: Are you free next Thursday? I need someone to attend parents evening

235

Tuesday, 18 May, Gloucester Road

It wasn't a crazy idea in theory. When I had met Felix's teacher Miss Lucas, it had felt like a more useful and honest conversation than she ever could have had with George and Beatriz. As a measure of parental pressure, it was about as far from the Northovers as I could hope to get. But I had only been back tutoring regularly in the holding pen for a few weeks. Was I really the best man for the job?

Arriving at the school's assembly hall, I felt like I'd come to a swingers' night, based on the number of looks I saw being traded between married couples. I made my way to my appointment with Mr Baxter — a kind-seeming man in his forties who I could imagine getting stuck with at a wedding reception while he talked earnestly for thirty minutes about the fact that he had once lived in Singapore.

'I haven't taught Emil much recently,' I said as I took a seat.

'Emil?' said Mr Baxter. 'Are you not here for Samir?'

He frowned and got on with telling me how Samir was doing in class. I made all the right noises — yes, you know the one — but it felt like we were reading from a script. I could tell Mr Baxter disapproved of the situation, if not me personally. Teachers at schools like this turned a blind eye to the remarkable consistency of their pupils' homework, but sending a tutor to parents' evening was crossing a line.

'Do you have any questions?' said Mr Baxter.

It was a cursory enquiry, but I barely even paused to think.

'Do you know where Samir's parents are? Are they even in the country?'

Mr Baxter looked completely astonished.

'I wouldn't have a clue.'

Of course he wouldn't. No one who hadn't been inside that house could begin to imagine the way it was run. I wanted to tell him all about it — from my mad first encounter with Emil to the mysterious drawer full of cash. But Mr Baxter seemed like he knew the wisdom of maintaining a sensible distance. Besides, our ten minutes were up.

Me:	Did you ever have a tutor turn up to parents evening?
Mum:	No. I did once have a sixth former who sat on her mother's lap.

Thursday, 20 May, Highgate

At last, Felix got called for interview. We had a lesson in the diary for the weekend, but Beatriz was so excited she insisted I come that day. After so many months of pent-up anxiety, the moment was here. Unfortunately

Felix wasn't. Beatriz had expected the driver to bring him home from school the same time as I arrived. But she had got her days mixed up. The driver had taken him to capoeira.

'Don't worry,' I said. 'I can come back tomorrow.'

'NO!' said Beatriz. 'Get in the car.'

I didn't understand why we wouldn't get the driver to bring Felix to us, but we leaped into the car and tore off at breakneck speed.

'Phone Gustav!' Beatriz cried. 'Get Felix OUT of that class!'

Gustav sounded alarmed when he picked up, as if he thought I might be calling to declare my love or arrange a date. Beatriz clarified matters by squawking instructions from the wheel. By the time we reached the capoeira studio, Felix was waiting outside.

'In!' Beatriz snapped. 'QUICK!'

Felix looked completely nonplussed, this not ranking that highly among the most deranged behaviour he had witnessed from his mother, maybe even that week.

'Go on, Matt,' Beatriz said.

I pulled a face.

'Get in the back. For the lesson!'

We'd be home in fifteen minutes. There was absolutely nothing we were going to achieve on the back seat of a BMW. But Beatriz wasn't capable of such a rational thought process, and Felix knew it as well as I did. For the remainder of the journey, we trotted over some facts we had already revised to the point of exhaustion. By the time we got home, there were only twenty minutes before I had to leave.

'Every second counts!' said Beatriz.

Felix and I retreated to the playroom. Once we sat down, he looked at me sadly.

'They fired Zoraida.'

I felt sick. He looked heartbroken. Then it came — a flood of tears that quickly escalated into full-on sobs. I said nothing and let it all come out. It felt like he had been holding it in for years.

'Please don't make me have another tutor,' Felix said eventually.

For a moment I wasn't sure of his logic. Did he think I was going to quit? No, he meant I was expendable, depending on the result of this test. He knew that if he failed it would not be tutoring, only my version of it that would be sent packing. Someone else would be brought in, and Felix would be stuck in the same miserable cycle — being catapulted through hoops while never learning how to jump.

Warren: Hello Matt! I'll see you outside the theatre at 7.15. I'm wearing a cravat :)

Zoe: He's wearing a cravat!!!

Saturday, 5 June, Covent Garden

Warren, the man from Jocasta's party, was taking me to
see a show. I told myself it wasn't a date. Sure, Warren
fancied me, but that didn't mean I couldn't interest
him in my work. I still hadn't actually finished a draft
of a short film script, but it was never too early to start
raising a budget, and this opportunity had fallen into
my lap. Maybe I had been wrong to discount the benefits
of being part of Jocasta's world.

Warren wanted to see the latest buzzy Sondheim
revival and had insisted on getting us a box. Judging
from his self-satisfied expression, which he maintained
even as the action descended into tragedy, the chance to
sit on display for two hours with a man twenty years his
junior was the evening's main appeal. I was happy for
Warren to get whatever he wanted from the occasion so
long as I was afforded a similar courtesy. After the show
we went for dinner at Joe Allen's, a restaurant so beloved
of theatre queens that there was literally a cast member
of the original production of *Cats* propping up the bar. I
wondered if they had her on retainer. Warren was keen to
learn what I had thought of the mezzo-soprano, but I was
barely able to criticise her vibrato before blurting out that
I was seeking investors in my short film. I had revealed
myself as an opportunist. Warren's face fell accordingly.

'I don't tend to fund individual projects,' he sniffed.

He explained that he preferred to support artists. His last
boyfriend had been a sculptor who Warren had assisted

financially to give him the time and space he needed to create. I listened in shock. Was this a proposition?

Warren paid the bill and walked me to the Tube. 'Oh,' he said, as if only just realising. 'My flat is right this way. Would you like a cup of tea?'

Here it was – my casting couch moment. Just like that, a possible future unfolded before my eyes. Within minutes, we would be making love in front of his baby grand. Afterwards we'd discuss my vision for my career. If I put my mind to it, I could have my film funded by sunrise. All I had to do was lie back and think about the backing dancers in *Sweeney Todd*.

'I won't,' I said to Warren. 'But thanks.'

Nadia: Both Emil's nannies are away on Saturday. Are you free to take him to the museum?

Saturday, 12 June, South Kensington

I should have known parents' evening wouldn't be the last of it. The appeal of the holding pen was how easily you could come and go, never knowing who you would be teaching or getting overwhelmed by a client's demands. But as soon as I had proved willing to overstep a boundary, Nadia had decided there was no limit to the roles in which you could employ a tutor. I promised myself this was a one-off.

241

I picked up Emil on his scooter and we headed to the museum. It was only then it occurred to me that I had been left in charge of a child who was travelling by vehicle while I was on foot. The route took us via an underground passage filled with tourists. As Emil sped ahead, gliding in and out of view, I felt like I was in a Liam Neeson film and that Emil could be swiped from under my nose by the bad guys at any moment (at least that's how I imagine it — obviously the only Liam Neeson film I've seen is *Love Actually*).

'One adult, one child,' I said to the woman at the ticket desk. She peered at Emil then at me with what felt like intense suspicion. I smiled down at Emil to assure the ticket lady of the propriety of our bond, but I was unsure whether to feign the warm, loving smile of a father or the competent, professional smile of a nanny. Deciding there was a high risk I'd accidentally feign the creepy and criminally suspect smile of a sex offender, I snatched the tickets and asked Emil where he wanted to start.

The dinosaur section was heaving with people. I was convinced Emil was about to burst into tears or wet himself and expose my lack of childcare skills. Instead he held my hand. He was captivated by the exhibits, creeping up to each giant model and gazing at it in awe. Was I overthinking this? Maybe I could be a positive presence in Emil's life without the intensity of the bond I shared with Felix. As Emil stood transfixed by a triceratops, a question occurred to him. He turned to me without thinking.

'Daddy?'

Friday, 18 June, Peckham

I had never been more certain that I needed to get away from this world and back into the life of a normal twenty-something. Maybe I'd find the answer on the roof of a car park in Peckham. A friend of mine who had a spare room going had invited me there to see his flatmates' band play. The car park had been turned into an art exhibition called Bold Tendencies, which sounded like something I might write in the report of a pupil who had a habit of farting. As I arrived at the exhibition and saw the work on display, I wasn't sure it had been accurately titled. One sculpture consisted entirely of concrete bricks, while another one left me unsure if it was an *objet d'art* or a pile of lost property.

'Watch out,' said Zoe. 'This place is full of wankers.'

But she knew as well as I did that we were two of them. A car park in Peckham might be a little more down at heel than Jocasta's Notting Hill mansion, but it was on the same continuum. I wouldn't have been surprised if one or two kids of Jocasta's friends were in attendance. By far the most pointed exhibit was the assembled crowd – a group of largely white middle class people drinking wine from tumblers while literally looking down on the Black locals of Peckham High Street.

My friend's band had the whole rooftop dancing, but seemed destined for chart obscurity with a name like Clean Bandit. Afterwards, Zoe and I sat looking out over a panorama which stretched from the local market

243

stalls to the skyscrapers of the financial district and the wealthier suburbs beyond.

'So do you think I should take the room?'

'Do I think you should move in with a group of really cool people your own age or stay living with a woman who has literally imposed a sex ban? Tough one.'

That cleared that up. I only wished it hadn't taken this long to arrive at what felt like a starting point. Maybe that was always the way. Zoe was making changes of her own — after three years of freelancing, she had got a job working full-time for a design studio. Aside from one boy she taught on Skype, she was retiring as a tutor.

'I'm going to miss having you as my tutoring buddy,' I said.

'You'll be fine,' said Zoe. 'You've got this.'

'That's the problem. I'm getting too good at this shit.'

Wednesday, 23 June, Highgate

Felix hadn't heard back from St Paul's. Beatriz had been at her wits' end ever since he was called in and was bombarding me with messages. It seemed unfair that I should have to deal with this in the one week I could no longer affect the outcome, but I should have known that the logical conclusion of giving her my number was a fourteen message stream of consciousness accompanied by a GIF of Dawson from *Dawson's Creek* bursting into tears. By the end of the week, Beatriz discovered brevity. A blunt text informed me of Felix's fate.

My first reaction was relief. I had failed at my job, but I had spared Felix five years in an environment which could have left his spirit permanently crushed. Beatriz did not feel similarly. Ten minutes later, she called me in a rage.

'I've identified the problem,' she said. 'You used the wrong textbook.'

God knows how she had come up with that one.

'I think they're all pretty similar, to be honest.'

Beatriz huffed, as if it was this lack of discernment that had got us here in the first place.

'Matt, how has this happened? We couldn't have prepared any harder. I thought you said he had an excellent chance.'

Now could have been the moment I spoke the truth. Reeling from defeat, maybe she would accept that there were greater factors in Felix's lack of success than my choice of textbook. Maybe she would even be open to the idea that this was a blessing in disguise. When I was Felix's age I was in my last year of primary school. I had never been set homework, never revised for exams and never felt any amount of pressure from my studies. But I hadn't missed out. It was Felix and so many kids like him who had been denied the tremendous sense of freedom and curiosity I'd had at that age. Instead they had been led to believe that everything is a competition and nothing is ever good enough — a mindset that would colour not only the rest of their lives, but anyone else they encountered.

This wasn't only something I'd observed in my pupils. After spending my teenage years at private school, I was uncomfortably familiar with this way of thinking.

Beatriz wasn't ready for that conversation. But I couldn't face it either. In my first year as a study buddy, I had been shocked by how much the parents left me to it, but that now felt like a healthier response than this obsessive and narrow-minded ambition which I didn't believe was in any child's best interests.

'I've got to go,' I said. 'I'm sorry it wasn't better news.'

As Beatriz hung up, I didn't think I'd ever hear from her again.

MIAMI

The original plan had been to spend the summer in Russia. Nicholas Nick was set to sit his Eton test that autumn, which meant that in theory, preparations would be taken up a gear. I spent the flight trying to figure out how guilty I felt about Felix. I knew I had done everything I could, but couldn't shake my belief that this was the best result for him. Maybe my crime was proceeding full steam with a project I had long since ceased to believe in.

As the plane landed in Moscow, the pilot announced a balmy temperature and I looked forward to that unmatched feeling when you step off a plane in a climate hotter than the one you departed. But when the moment arrived, it came with a sting. The air prickled with smoke as if there was a bonfire nearby.

'No nice study for boys,' was Maria's impeccable diagnosis.

Russia was gripped by wildfires. I had read about them before taking off, but I hadn't realised their effects could be felt in Moscow. The fires were causing havoc for Sergei's agricultural operation and he was busier than ever trying to handle it. But Maria couldn't hide her delight. We had to escape the inferno.

'Maybe Greece?' Maria said as if idly selecting a breakfast cereal. 'Or Maldives?'

I made it clear that these were not locations to which I had any objections, but didn't take entirely seriously a woman who had previously fantasised about conversation lessons in Bali. When she came to me a few days later and said she had found a solution, I assumed she meant some expensive type of air conditioner. But no — we were going to Miami.

Zoe: You are the jammiest little fucker I have
          ever met

My late introduction to air travel meant there was no part of departure lounges and security checks I didn't find just a bit exciting. There was something satisfying about settling into that vaguely grumpy travel mood — the one that allows you to enjoy almost any in-flight movie, no matter how bad. It had nothing in common with the jaunty performance I gave as a tutor. We were being joined on our trip by Titty Piggy, and while I was looking forward to a Piggy reunion, the prospect of a twelve-hour flight with a client was exhausting. Arriving at the airport, I found that the Piggies were the least of my worries.

'Matt,' said Maria. 'Meet Anya and Victor.'

'Victor Babkov,' said Victor, stepping forward. 'I'm Sergei's friend.'

'His art advisor,' said Maria, dismissing any claim of friendship with her husband.

'Yes, I sell him lots of paintings,' said Victor. 'Very good price.'

By the look of Victor's designer sunglasses, it was a price that worked for him too. I didn't know if Victor always dressed like a low-level Florida crime boss or had tailored his outfit for the trip based on reruns of *Miami Vice*. Anya had an air of glamour about her, but for the flight was wearing a type of flannel leggings that were tight around the legs but so loose around the bum that they resembled a soiled nappy. I wasn't sure why this pair were joining our party — was Anya the real friend and Victor the price we had to pay? Or had Sergei ensured we didn't jet halfway across the world without sending along Uncle Piggy to keep an eye on me and his wife? As we boarded the plane, I was desperate to get away from Victor and plugged into some mediocre Kate Hudson romcom. Naturally I ended up sitting next to him. I tried swapping seats with Anya, who was next to an extremely attractive Italian. This hadn't been lost on Anya, who insisted she was happy to be separated from her beloved. We were still on the runway when Victor began pontificating on the subtleties of the art market and explaining complex concepts such as auctions.

Maria leaned over. 'Victor — Matt went to Cambridge.'

Since she saw me as a branded accessory that she was taking on holiday, much like her Gucci handbag, there was no point unless the brand name was prominently displayed. Victor looked at me accusingly.

'Do you have a girlfriend?'

I confessed that I didn't, thrilled to have so quickly found an arena where Victor had me trumped. But this wasn't enough for him. He pulled out his phone and showed me increasingly intimate photos of Anya, including one of her lying on a bed in expensive lingerie, clutching bundles of euros.

'She very very like money,' he explained.

The next photo featured Victor awkwardly straddling Anya on a quad bike in the desert. 'Did you ever did quadricycle?' he asked.

'I've done it many times,' Nicholas Nick chipped in. 'Got it, done it, got a T-shirt.'

'You got a T-shirt?' said Victor. 'When?'

As we landed in Miami and drove away from the airport, we passed whole streets where homes had been marked for foreclosure. The neighbourhoods got gradually more upmarket, and soon we arrived at the entrance to West Palm Residential Community. A fountain and flower beds did their best to soften the edges of a fortified security barrier and a guard with a gun mounted on his hip. The guard peered into our vehicle, but Maria was the kind of person whose wealth dripped from every pore.

'Good afternoon, ma'am,' purred the guard. 'Welcome to West Palm.'

A gated community wasn't a typical place for holiday rentals, but I imagine the crash had left it with more available property than desired. Driving through the entrance, it felt like we had entered a scene from *Stepford Wives*. Identical homes were set back from the road behind perfectly manicured lawns. There were several gardeners at work who must have been at it non-stop to keep every blade of grass so trim. Our house was a peach-coloured mansion that looked like it had been designed in crayon by children then built in a week. The interior was overstuffed with statement furniture in a way suited to Maria's tastes. But she looked around with a frown. 'Is not big enough, no?'

It looked more than ample to me. But I was speaking to a woman whose garage had two floors and its own shower. Maria made a call to Sergei, and twenty minutes later we had been upgraded to one of the community's 'premium' properties. It didn't matter how much I had learned to think like a rich person — there was always another level. From now on, I would not get out of bed to tutor for less than six en-suite bedrooms and an underground gym.

You had to admire a woman who had flown us halfway round the world in search of the optimum study conditions. The irony was that Nicholas Nick could have got into Eton if we'd done our revision in a lay-by on the M27. He didn't need a whole month of lessons, but tutors are rarely incentivised to talk themselves out of a job.

Instead, I resolved to expand Nicholas Nick's knowledge. For that, we turned to a quiz website called Sporcle.

'Burkina Faso?'

'Ouagadougou.'

'Sri Lanka?'

'Sri Jayawardenepura Kotte.'

Nicholas Nick learned every capital city of the world within days. We moved on to the ceremonial counties of England, which it would have been nice to think was my area of expertise. It quickly became clear that I am better equipped to give a TED talk on the ins and outs of hedge funds than locate Bedfordshire on a map or tell you what, let alone where, Rutland is.

'Good studies, boys?'

It was Victor Babkov. It was no surprise that this esteemed scholar had dropped in on our studies, but he had picked the wrong moment to massage his ego.

'I bet you don't know the capital of Sri Lanka,' said Nicholas Nick with a grin.

Victor looked mortified. He paused, determined not to give in but unsure how to proceed. He put a finger to his ear, and for a terrible moment I thought he was going to pretend he hadn't heard the question. But it was only a nervous tic. Then a sense of calm flooded his face. What followed was the most ingenuity I ever witnessed in Victor Babkov.

'Nice try,' he said. 'Look it up yourself!'

Then he mimed strangling Nicholas Nick, and we all laughed.

It was tempting to toy with a man like Victor Babkov, but the only advisable strategy was to avoid him whenever possible. Unfortunately Maria had other plans. 'Stimulation for boys' was how she described it. While this created a mental image I would prefer never to have had, I was relieved to learn that all she meant was a motivational activity to get me and Nicholas Nick to the end of the week.

'Maybe we can rent a yacht,' said Maria, looking at a brochure emblazoned with the words YACHTS FOR RENT. But Victor was determined to have a better idea.

'Yes,' he said. 'Or jump from a helicopter.'

Maria murmured politely, but it did seem to be just yachts that were on offer in this particular brochure. Victor paused for a long time.

'Maybe we can roll down the beach in a giant inflatable ball.'

Maria looked at him in the way you might at a three-year-old who had just suggested a picnic on the moon.

'Yes,' she said. 'Maybe.'

A few days later, we drove to a marina filled with huge, shiny boats. Ours had a crew of five led by Captain Felipe, a sun-beaten local who appeared to rather enjoy wearing his crisp white uniform and certainly had no objections to his kinky white gloves. The other crew members were in polo shirts, apart from Chef Salvador who, presumably under contract, wore one of those chef's hats which left him ready at any moment to be cast in a Disney cartoon. It was well within my nature to attempt some embarrassingly jovial friendship with one or more of the staff of the type they no doubt yawn through on a weekly basis. As it turned out, I wouldn't get the chance.

The back of the boat had a sun deck that made me wish I was an A-list celebrity at risk of getting papped with my hot new rumoured lover. I closed my eyes and imagined the tabloid headlines. Then a shadow fell over me.

'Beer?' said Victor, offering me one.

I declined, but he looked crestfallen. 'Go on then,' I said.

Victor perked up immediately. 'Do you know this?' he asked, before attempting to remove the lid of the beer bottle with his teeth. I presume he intended it as one swift action, but on this occasion he was unable. He resorted to holding the bottle with both hands, clamping down his jaw and yanking hard.

'Shall I get that for you?' asked a horrified staff member.

'No, no,' said Victor through gritted teeth. It was clear to everyone on the sun deck that even if he succeeded in removing the lid, he would at best be handing me a bottle drenched in his saliva, and at worst would require medical attention.

'Bingo!' Victor said, which was one way of putting it. He handed me the bottle, in some pain. But the real torture was yet to begin. Victor had arrived at his main purpose, which was convincing me I was in the presence of an intellectual. His strategy involved informing me of some random piece of knowledge, then commenting 'I bet they didn't teach you that at Cambridge.' Invariably this was true, though I'm sure those who compile the Spanish and Italian syllabuses have their reasons for not including a module on the Russian Civil War.

Lunch was served on the sun deck on a crisp white tablecloth that I imagined greatly pleased Captain Felipe. I hadn't planned on sitting next to Anya. Much as Victor rarely conversed with her himself, I couldn't be bothered with the repercussions if he thought I was taking an interest in his girlfriend or vice versa. But today we found ourselves side by side. There was only one thing Anya wanted me to know about her, which was that she was a dog breeder.

'Ooh, what type of dog?'

'It's called . . . Germany . . .'

'German shepherd?'

'No. Germany dog.'

A cross reference between Anya's photo library and Google confirmed that she did mean German shepherd. But nothing would shake her from her belief that the correct term was Germany dog.

'My dog is ranked fourteen in the world,' she told me proudly, though it was not clear in what discipline fourteen or more Germany dogs are internationally ranked. She showed me a series of videos of her and her prize hounds at the Germany Dog World Championships. This clarified nothing.

After lunch, I was napping on a sun lounger when I felt someone approach.

'Do you like ping pong?' asked Victor.

I should have known that Maria wouldn't settle for any yacht which didn't include a ping pong table. I don't like ping pong, especially not after a boozy lunch in the middle of the ocean, but my dalliance with Anya was bound to incur some punishment and it might as well be this. I assumed Victor wanted to thrash me and I was happy to let him, but as he urged Anya to come and watch and began cracking jokes, I realised his goal was even more tragic. He wanted her to know that our fraternal connection was deeper than anything she and I had shared at lunch.

Anya barely looked up from her phone. Deflated, Victor's game fell apart. Each time he hit a poor shot he made a big show of examining his bat, as though it were that which had caused the error. I found myself imagining him doing the same with his penis after another round of disappointing intercourse with Anya. Before the match was up, I had renamed him Victor Badcock.

I was thrilled to learn that Victor and Anya were only staying a week. The gated community had various in-house restaurants where we ate most nights, but to celebrate — I mean lament — Victor and Anya's departure, we dressed up and drove into town. Entering the city, we passed a gay bar packed with a lively Friday night crowd. It was so easy in the company of clients to convince yourself that this was your reality, nowhere more so than in a gated community that literally shut out any intrusions from the outside world. But the moment you looked around, you caught glimpses of the life you were missing.

Maria had booked a private room at a busy Italian restaurant. Just as in Moscow, I wasn't convinced by her approach to fine dining. Surely part of the fun of eating out was being surrounded by other diners and changing your order at the last minute because you were jealous of the woman at the next door table's cannelloni. Knowing I was going to be free of Victor tomorrow, I felt I could indulge him for one more night, and sat through a mind-numbing monologue on Damien bloody Hirst. He came up so often in these circles that I was convinced if I had bitched about him more consistently I could have crashed the international art market.

When we got to the end of the meal, Maria leaned in with a smile.

'Do you know that Matt can sing?'

I knew exactly what she was thinking, since she had told the story a thousand times of our trip to famed Moscow karaoke joint Who Is Who. But that was the kind of triumph you couldn't plan. Didn't Maria know lightning doesn't strike twice?

'Matt, do "O Mio Babbino Caro".'

It was the most ostentatious number she could have chosen.

'No,' I wanted to say. 'That was a treat for Mummy Piggy.'

My protests fell on deaf ears. I began to perform in as low key a manner as you can when you are a man singing Puccini in falsetto. But there was no avoiding the fact that Victor's farewell dinner had turned into a concert performance by the tutor who had beaten him at ping pong. Victor formed a rictus of a smile and held it firm. It lasted until Anya got out her phone and began to film me.

Afterwards, Victor couldn't hide his disgust.

'How can you not be married?' he despaired. 'You are twenty-four, smart, sport *and* good-looking.'

Inadvertently I had got to the heart of Victor Babkov. His anger went beyond the bounds of my personal situation. He was cross at something larger — a world in which attributes of perceived desirability did not lead to expected outcomes in matrimony. Maria looked at me with an amused smile.

'Victor is two times divorced.'

I can't say it wasn't a relief to have Victor gone. But I quickly realised I was *grateful* to him for sucking up all the attention. Now that the moment had arrived, I didn't have the energy to resume the role of Daddy Piggy. It was the first time I'd properly enjoyed myself as a tutor, and my affection for Maria was real. But it was still a role. Every night at the gated community we went through the same charade of thinking about going to their seafood restaurant for dinner before deciding we preferred their French bistro. But that night, at the last minute, I told Maria I felt like seafood and went the opposite way.

West Palm was a self-styled 'family-oriented' development, and a young man dining alone attracted looks of suspicion. At least there were no Northovers to judge me — I could order anything I wanted and add it to Maria's tab. The most expensive item on the menu was lobster thermidor. It was one of those dishes, like frogs' legs or caviar, that I was aware of as a child. Not from restaurants — my parents were very conscious of the cost of eating out as a family of six. It was in books and TV shows that I first became aware of these signifiers of wealth. Then aged twelve, I started attending private school. Suddenly this world was tantalisingly within reach.

Is that why I had been so drawn to tutoring? At school I had seen first hand how the other half lived, but I had been an outsider, at least when it came to money. They even had a name for us — staff kids. I was no less an outsider as a tutor, but far more of a welcome one. Clients flew me round the world and treated me like a family member. But treated who? Hiding my sexuality was the least of it. In order to succeed as a tutor I had tacitly endorsed my clients' values and turned a blind eye to their behaviour. Was that so different to a freeloader like Victor Babkov? Maybe we had more in common than I wanted to admit.

As I walked home from the restaurant, drunk on margaritas, the heavens opened. Rainstorms in Florida were short and sharp, but I didn't take shelter. I began to walk slower, relishing the sensation of getting soaked to my skin. A car passed and I saw the woman at the wheel stare at me. This was the kind of experience you weren't meant to have in a place like this, where even nature was manipulated to deny its rough edges. The woman clearly thought I was insane. But unlike anyone else that week, she was seeing the real me.

YEAR THREE

AUTUMN TERM 2010

Tuesday, 7 September, Chelsea

Philippa had asked me to come in for a meeting. It was two years since I had seen her in person and I could barely recall the clueless version of myself I had been. It wasn't only me who had changed. The agency had moved into swanky new offices, expanded its staff fourfold and begun inviting me to dubious events about mindfulness and educational psychology. It was odd that Philippa had asked to meet, and while I had sufficiently matured not to assume I was in trouble, I couldn't think what it was about.

'Good news,' said Philippa. 'We've made you a prefect.'

She had always had strong head girl energy, but this was taking private school cosplay to a new level.

'Mmm,' I said. 'What does that mean?'

Philippa looked surprised, as if she existed in a world where the honour of being made a prefect was self-evident.

'It'll go on your tutor profile,' she said. 'Parents will see it. But that's not what I wanted to discuss.'

She was as excited as I had ever seen her, and I realised that whatever she was planning to offer, the prefectship was a mere *amuse bouche*.

'It's a real game changer for the industry,' said Philippa. 'It's something I've been looking at doing for the past few years.'

She took a deep breath.

'I'm offering you the chance to become a professional tutor.'

I looked blank.

'So what does that make me now?'

Philippa didn't crack a smile.

'What I mean is — we're planning to employ tutors on a salary.'

A salary. The golden goose.

'You'd get a pension. The works.'

A pension! My parents might be relaxed about raising unsalaried children, but I knew they would be delighted if they thought I had given even the slightest consideration to the concept of a pension.

'How much are we talking?'

If Philippa could write a number on a pad of paper and make my eyes widen like they do in Hollywood films, maybe I could get on board with this salary concept.

'It would be in line with other professional careers,' she said tartly.

I should have seen this coming. I had always been amazed at how willing the tutoring industry had been to throw large sums of money at cowboys like me.

'We think this would make you among the leading tutors in the country.'

I was perfectly happy with my current status as one of the country's leading unprofessional tutors. But the further I got into adulthood and saw my Facebook enemies going on expensive holidays and putting down flat deposits, the more I saw the appeal of things like pensions and salaries. Then I remembered my short film. I no longer thought it was going to make me the toast of Hollywood, but I'd had an idea about who could produce it and was determined not to let tutoring get in the way of my creative ambitions this year. I told Philippa I'd think about it.

Max:	Hey guys, did someone eat my leftover curry? I was saving that for tonight
Me:	Shit. Sorry! Feel free to have one of my bean soups
Max:	I'm good

Wednesday, 22 September, Shoreditch

Aside from the occasional hiccup, life with my new flat-mates was going well. Most of them were freelancers but all in different fields, which meant there was none of the competitiveness I was liable to let consume me. I was hoping to start my tutoring for the year with a similarly clean slate. Then I saw that Carolyn, my favourite Kensington blogger, was calling. I had helped Horace with his coursework and Arthur with choral singing, but there wasn't a third child and I couldn't imagine why Carolyn was getting in touch. I have a terrible inability to let a phone ring. Something convinces me it must be important and there will be terrible consequences if I don't pick up.

'Matt, so nice to hear your voice,' said Carolyn. 'How are you?'

Actually I was in bed with a friend of a friend who I had accompanied to a Lady Gaga gig the previous night. Freed from Jocasta's flagship policy, I had invited my gig companion back to mine to reimburse him the £50 I owed him for the ticket. I knew there was a reason I shouldn't have picked up the phone.

'Fine thanks,' I said to Carolyn. 'How are you?'

'Busy, Matt, busy.'

Carolyn was the kind of woman who liked to be extremely busy at all times, so that her darkest thoughts only came to her at 4 a.m., which in any case was around the time she got up to knock out 400 words for her blog on the decline in quality of the local cheesemonger.

'Remind me, Matt — did you go to Oxford or Cambridge?'

I reminded her, already fearing where this was heading.

'I was at Oxford myself, of course,' Carolyn said. 'So I know what it's like.'

Of course? Was I meant to know her complete life history? Or did she feel it was a fact that made sense to all who encountered her? She began grilling me on my degree as if she was an examiner, if the examiner was extremely intellectually insecure and felt the need to make clear how acquainted *they* were with each author I mentioned.

'How are you on the Renaissance, Matt? Horace has been really getting into his Boccaccio.'

She said the name with a pseudo-authentic twang, and I knew instantly that she used the same accent when ordering at Carluccio's, specifically choosing one of the more obscure pastas because it gave her a better chance to show off. It was then I realised Carolyn had said something which probably wasn't best answered by me doing an impression of her saying the word *farfadelle*.

'Sorry, could you say that again? The line cut out.'

'Of course,' said Carolyn. 'Horace is applying to Oxford.'

Dear tutors,
We are looking for volunteers to conduct practice Oxbridge interviews at an academy in Hackney.
Former sink school, but turned around in very impressive fashion by Sir Richard Dunbar, who is now head of Ofsted.
Let me know if you are interested,
　　Philippa

Saturday, 2 October, Hackney

I had seen the email a week or two earlier and done nothing about it. Now it felt like fate. I had known from the start that my tutoring career wasn't going to win me a Pride of Britain award. But Oxbridge entrance was a straight-up competition between those who had been preparing for this moment their whole lives and those who were thrown in at the deep end. I had always avoided the jobs when they came up, but my compulsion to answer the phone was matched by my inability to say no to a client. Rather than feel vaguely guilty, it was time to put my money where my mouth was by leaving money out of the equation for once.

When I looked up the academy in question, I found that not only had its former head been knighted, it was now based in a £20 million building which had been commissioned from a noted architect by an educational philanthropist, both of whom were also ennobled. I was a little suspicious of any educational reforms that boosted the fortunes of more white men with knighthoods than individual schools, but I suppose there were worse ways for knights to spend their time.

There were two girls interested in studying languages. Tameka was confident and enthusiastic, but Fatima stood out immediately. Her parents were born in a village in Turkey where a university education wasn't a consideration, let alone Cambridge. But Fatima's personal statement was a thing of beauty. She wrote about everything from the circularity of time in Latin American literature to the political symbolism of bread in the poems of Gabriela Mistral. She even quoted El Cid, which I was mainly impressed by because it was a name I had been meaning to look up for several years and hadn't known until now whether it was a person or a book.

'So how would you define the idea of circular time?' I asked Fatima.

In my head, I heard Felix make some sardonic quip about a clock, but Fatima just giggled and shrugged.

'You gave quite a good definition in your statement.'

'Oh, did I? I'm not sure.'

I started to wonder if she'd actually written the thing. But as it became clear that she had, I realised her lack of confidence was the problem. You could see her grow self-conscious in real time, as her sharp instincts became a mess of nerves. I wanted to help her but I didn't know how. And unlike Horace, whose mother had scheduled weekly lessons until December, this was the only session we had arranged.

'Thanks for giving up your precious time,' the organiser said as we were shown out. 'We'll let you know how they get on.'

Soraya: Hey, I'm free at 6 today. Jake can meet us at 6.30.

Me: Perfect. Half an hour on the bean bags, half an hour in the canteen?

Thursday, 7 October, Victoria

Soraya was a friend I had taken classes with at uni. She now worked at Google, but she'd helped set up a film festival and I had a feeling she'd make a great producer. Not only had she said yes, she'd immediately cracked on with launching a crowdfunder. I intended to make the most of my good fortune. For Soraya, Google was a convenient place for us to meet after work. For me, it was like holding pre-production on the International Space Station. As well as the bean bags, the office had a free canteen with chef-prepared meals and a snack bar stocked better than any Pret. If we were going to make a cinematic masterpiece, it was important to have complimentary access to an unlimited supply of coconut water.

'Right,' said Soraya as I wolfed down a lamb medallion. 'Where are we at with the script?'

Soraya had suggested I focus on only one aspect of my heart-wrenching drama set in the cut-throat worlds of animal smuggling and gay adoption. For several reasons, gay adoption made most sense, so I went with animal smuggling. The new story revolved around a reptile breeder and his girlfriend, a role for which we were attempting to woo an arthouse actress. She wasn't a household name but had some very impressive credits, so I tended to refer to her like an overexcited awards host as 'Star of the Palme d'Or-winning *4 Months, 3 Weeks and 2 Days*, BAFTA Award Winner Anamaria Marinca'.

270

'Anamaria's agent read it,' Soraya said. 'She liked it, but found some parts confusing.'

'It's *meant* to be confusing.'

Soraya gave me a look which reminded me that my most valuable instinct as a director was knowing how desperately I needed a producer. I cracked into a muesli yoghurt and we discussed a couple of ways of making the script a little more comprehensible. Halfway through the yoghurt we were joined by Jake, a cinematographer who had expressed an interest in the project but had a few questions. I resisted the urge to tell him that was exactly what I had intended.

'Are you planning to storyboard?' Jake asked.

I glanced at Soraya. I wasn't 100% sure what story-boarding was, though I had a vague memory from my visit to Conrad's studio of seeing some hand-drawn images of Ali, Genie and PIG.

'Definitely,' I said.

Soraya clocked Jake's reaction and realised that any attempts to pull the wool over his eyes were destined to fail.

'This is our first film.'

I opened my mouth then closed it, sensing that it wouldn't help matters to boast of my on-set experience on 'Ali and the Lamp', starring an actual piglet as PIG.

'That's fine,' said Jake. 'I like working with new talent.'

'Great,' said Soraya. 'Shall we discuss the chameleon?'

Zoe: Thank you so much for doing this! I
            promise, easiest client ever

Monday, 11 October, Shoreditch

Soon after starting her new job, Zoe had realised she didn't have time to keep the one kid she taught on Skype — a British boy at an international school in Malaysia. I was happy to take him off her hands, since locating myself on a different continent to my pupil felt like another way to get some distance from tutoring. It was a doddle, Zoe promised. 'You don't even need to put your trousers on!'

I assumed that wasn't her official advice. It seemed a bad idea to interact with a child over the internet wearing nothing but a pair of pants on your bottom half. The point was that I didn't have to leave the house. Jasper's parents were worried his English was slipping, but Zoe claimed the tutoring was only to ease their guilt and required little more than setting Jasper the odd compre-hension. On the day of the call I checked several times I was wearing trousers, then dialled in. A grainy video popped up of Jasper and his mother Jane.

'Hi Matt, how are you?' said Jane.

I was horrified. It wasn't the sight of them, but myself. It is a curiously accepted fact of video corre-spondence that you are provided with a real-time image of yourself as well as your interlocutor. Humans have always managed face-to-face interactions without this aid, and I'm sure most would agree that if there was a mirror placed next to anyone we had a conversation with, that's where our attention would go.

'Our connection's not great,' said Jane. 'You keep freezing.'

It wasn't the best time for her to be talking to me, since I was in the middle of an existential crisis. This was far from my first Skype call, but it was my first as a tutor, and it made me hyper-conscious of the image on my screen. Who *was* he? This polite, compliant man, older than I liked to imagine, less attractive and far more serious. Fuck! Is this what people had been seeing all these years?

'Sorry about that, Jane,' I said. 'Let's switch to audio.'

Audio was a game changer. Rather than the sense of vigilance a video call creates, it liberated me and left me free to focus on the task at hand. I set Jasper off on a comprehension, then got on with my Tesco order. I needed to do a big shop for a house-warming party, and if I was efficient I could have everything in my basket by the time Jasper completed question six. I was flying through my list when I got to the hummus. There were more varieties than I expected, and I paused to decide if my guests would prefer Moroccan or jalapeño.

'Finished!' Jasper called out.

I was tempted to ignore the little gremlin, or at least pretend my audio had cut out. But I was not a fool. Tutoring in person, you were aware of whether or not a parent was in earshot. On Skype, it was impossible to know if someone was lurking round the corner.

'That's great,' I said to Jasper. Then something started flashing on my screen. It was a countdown telling me I needed to complete my order if I wanted to keep my delivery slot.

'Now read through your answers,' I said. 'And don't rush!'

Hi Matt,
We're inviting some of our more senior tutors to join our training sessions to make sure you're all up to date. Let me know which one suits.
    Philippa

None of those dates work for me, I'm afraid. I'll look out for the next lot.
    Matt

Wednesday, 13 October, North Kensington

A *senior* tutor? *Por favor*. I could only admire Philippa's efforts to professionalise her operation. But two jobs in a row had come via my own connections. I still got the agency's job alerts, but now I saw straight through the spin. If a child was described as energetic, you could be sure that within minutes of walking through the door they would be holding you hostage with a Nerf gun.

With Horace, I knew what I was letting myself in for. He was applying to read English and Italian, but not even his carefully worded personal statement could convince me his interest was sincere. I was sure that writing it had involved a structured seminar series, a specialist consultant who claimed a dubious percentage success rate on their personal website, and some lusty arguments with his mother about whether or not to include the word 'indubitably'.

Horace hadn't changed much in the past two years, but had grown his hair long and acquired some wrist-bands in a way that made him look too cool for school but perfect for a gap year in Malawi. We were holding a mock interview as a way for me to assess how bad the damage was.

'Why do you want to study literature?' I asked him.

'Because I . . . like books?' Horace said.

I suggested he be more specific, and we narrowed it down to Shakespeare. I noted that this was an interesting example to cite in his love of literature, considering the more traditional method of digesting Shakespeare's texts. Horace was unable to digest my point.

'Can you give me a definition of tragedy?' I asked.

This was basic stuff, but I was clutching at straws.

'It's kind of like . . . something sad.'

He would have been better off simply answering no.

I moved on to Italian, hoping he might sound more original on a subject not widely taught in schools. His

275

statement mentioned the frescoes painted by Giotto in the Scrovegni Chapel, which Carolyn informed me they had visited on a recent family holiday. I asked Horace to describe the experience.

'Well, we rented a villa near Verona for my dad's fiftieth, so—'

'The frescoes, Horace.'

'Oh, right. It's weird, because outside the chapel is kind of normal, but inside, it's like . . . friendly?'

It wasn't that his observation was fundamentally wrong. But Horace had not only visited the works in question, he'd had an art history tutor walk him through their various artistic and historical contexts in twelve pages of notes, which his mother — if I may boldly conjecture — had made him copy out on coloured cards. 'Normal on the outside, friendly on the inside' sounded less like the well-drilled analysis of a potential Oxford student than a toddler's assessment of Professor Dumbledore.

'Does he have a chance?' Carolyn asked me after the lesson. My answer came not from a desire to please my client, but a vivid memory of just how many people like Horace I had encountered at Cambridge.

'Oh yes,' I said.

Me:	I don't understand how these people make it past the interview
Zoe:	Then you have way too much faith in who's interviewing them

Saturday, 30 October, Covent Garden

My family were meeting at a pizza restaurant in London for my mum's birthday. It was also a chance for them to meet Julien, the Swiss man who had been asleep in my bed when Carolyn called. Against all odds, he was now my boyfriend. Even more surprising was the fact that I had some positive career news to share. After years of contacting every production company in existence, I had scored a job writing educational scripts for a YouTube channel. The films weren't going to win any awards, but it was paid work as a screenwriter. Slowly but surely, the chaos of the post-uni years was beginning to fade.

Since it was the other end of the student experience where my tutoring efforts were currently focused, I asked my parents if they had any interview tips for Fatima.

'She just doesn't have any confidence,' I said.

'That's the least of it,' said my dad.

He had recently been made chairman of governors at an academy much less well connected than the one Fatima studied at. The school had never had a pupil apply to Oxbridge, let alone get in.

'It's a totally different mentality,' said my dad. 'Lots of them can't even think about going to university away from home.'

I wondered if I had been blinkered for the past few years by focusing on younger kids. As soon as you saw the disparities in life outcomes, it was hard not to feel depressed.

'It's good of you to be volunteering,' said my mum. 'Is this your effect, Julien?'

I let Julien take the credit, happy for anything which cast him in a positive light. But I knew this new, wholesome image of me as a tutor wouldn't hold up for long. I admitted my general approach to Skype tutoring.

'Nice,' said my sister, who had recently started her teacher training, sealing my reputation as the quack of the family. 'Your pupils are so lucky to have you.'

'What happened to that other boy?' asked my mum. 'The one with his own cinema.'

I hadn't heard from the Northovers since my conversation with Beatriz. That didn't mean they hadn't been on my mind. Being effectively paid to be Felix's friend struck me as weirder than ever now that it had been terminated with an abrupt phone call. I wasn't sure if I went as far as missing him, but I certainly wondered how he was doing. Part of me hoped he had been freed from the treadmill of tutoring. Another part of me hated the thought of him having to go it alone.

Me: Thank you so much for doing this!
Zoe: Are you kidding? I can't wait

Saturday, 20 November, Hackney

I hadn't been able to stop thinking about Fatima. She was exactly the type of person who'd thrive at Cambridge, but for that she had to ace the interview and I was desperate to improve her chances. I offered to come back in for a second session, but this time I brought reinforcements. Not only was Zoe far more experienced than me with teenage girls, she had gone to a state school herself and I knew her advice would carry a weight for Fatima that mine never could. We went to the academy together and Zoe spoke to Fatima while I gave Tameka one more practice run. Then it was my turn with Fatima.

The interview was two weeks away but her nerves were already at the surface. This was what I was expecting, so I had googled interview tips to see if there was anything useful to pass on. Advice for the night beforehand ranged from shaving your legs and deep conditioning your hair to the ominous reminder to lay out your supplies. On the day, turning up early was a popular tip, though one website had provided a confusing template answer to explain your actions to the secretary. 'I'm very early,' you were supposed to announce. 'But I don't want to bother Alyssa Smith so far in advance.' (The invention of this imaginary Alyssa Smith character only made things more confusing.) You were then to offer to remind the secretary when it was closer to 2 p.m., which seemed a surefire way to make an enemy before you'd begun. Another website advised running around to get yourself out of breath, though it wasn't clear if you were supposed to do this before turning up early, or pop in to announce that you didn't want to bother Alyssa Smith, then head back out for a quick jog.

For the interview itself, the advice got even more bizarre. It ranged from making sure your hands were visible to leaning slightly forward on your chair, all of which was meant to be done while staying in your body, for anyone planning not to. The most striking tip was to open your throat by sticking your tongue out and reciting the entirety of 'Humpty Dumpty', at least until I realised I had misread and this was recommended for before and not during the interview.

There was only so much I could achieve in two sessions in the face of competitors who had spent their lives being made to believe they were entitled to a place. I tried to at least leave Fatima feeling inspired.

'Any last tips?' her teacher said to Zoe and me as he came to wrap things up.

Given that I couldn't think much beyond remembering to deep condition and staying the hell away from Alyssa Smith, I decided to sit this one out.

'Just be yourself,' Zoe said. 'The only thing these interviewers have to decide is whether they want to teach you for three years. You don't have to know everything. You just have to show them you want to learn.'

Saturday, 4 December, Clapton

I couldn't decide what I feared most — Horace getting an offer, or Fatima not. Worst of all would be the double whammy. Like someone who flies round the world making token donations towards their carbon footprint, it was wishful thinking that my less honourable endeavours could be so easily offset. I was anxiously awaiting news when I got a text from Maria:

I'll come UK on Saturday. I'll call u darling. Big kiss.

Presumably she'd missed a comma, though it would have been no surprise for her to call me darling, nor to announce it in advance. Maria added that she had a surprise, and while I was fairly sure what it was, I was happy to let her enjoy the suspense. The day beforehand, she hadn't revealed a time or location, and I texted asking where we should meet. A short while later, I got a reply:

See you in Clapton Pond!!!

I was going to need some more information. I still only had Saturday as a timescale, and I wasn't particularly keen to head to Clapton Pond early on and wait around. More pressingly, Clapton Pond was not an address, or even an area. It was a pond. Despite her instruction, I had to assume Maria didn't want to meet me *in* the pond

— though given the mystery surrounding the occasion, this may have been presumptuous.

Eventually I got an address out of her. Clapton was not where I would expect an oligarch's wife to stay while in London, but there was a long-winded explanation which I stopped trying to follow once it became clear — and that is a generous term — that it involved a man she had met at a clay pigeon shooting range in Hemel Hempstead. Maria had been joined by Nicholas Nick, who had come out of school for the weekend. She had filled the house with helium balloons and a Smurf piñata, and since I knew it wasn't any of our birthdays, I had narrowed down the surprise to two options, one of which was the unlikely possibility that I had been invited to a party for the man Maria had met at a clay pigeon shooting range in Hemel Hempstead. But my first suspicion was correct.

'Miätt!' Maria said as I walked through the door. 'Nikita make place in Eton!'

Thursday, 9 December, Shoreditch

A few days later, Fatima got an offer. Unsurprisingly, helping a state-educated Muslim girl get into Cambridge felt markedly more satisfying than profiting off the exploitative labour practices of the Russian dairy industry to get an oligarch's son into Eton. The next day, there was more good news. Horace had failed to be offered a place. It was the result all three deserved, meaning I was the lucky one.

The results had the sense of an ending. There would be no more trips to Russia, and I didn't plan on taking Carolyn's calls ever again. The problem was that there was a very small gap between relief at no longer having to deal with a client and worry about where my next job was coming from. I was going to have to go crawling back to Philippa, maybe even endure the humiliation of a tutor training session.

The next day when I woke up, I had three missed calls from Beatriz.

KENYA

'Watch out for baboons,' said Lando.

'Or giant snails,' added Caspian.

'Why would he need to watch out for those?'

'No, but you can see them.'

I had been picked up at the airport in a Jeep by two of Felix's cousins. I got the impression the task had been assigned to Lando and Caspian as the kind of responsible adult activity the brothers desperately needed. It was a good idea, since society can struggle to know what to do with highly privileged people lacking an obvious skill set, other than appoint them as working royals. The boys were in their late teens, with glowing tans which inspired such a jealous lust that it was comforting to think of it as irreversible sun damage. We had recently turned off the main road onto a private dirt track, and the brothers were competing to list storks, monkeys and other creatures I might glimpse in what had rapidly become a tantalising menagerie.

I was as surprised as anyone to be in Kenya for new year. When I spoke to Beatriz, she had acted as if our previous conversation had never happened. They had found a new school for Felix, and it was inconceivable that anyone other than me would help him prepare. It was like being contacted by an ex. Even with only a term's distance from the Northovers, I felt like a different person. But I was protective over Felix. If he was going to be put through the admissions wringer again, I wanted the person by his side to be me.

As we reached an open vista, the land stretched out beyond comprehension. Grassy plains and scrubland rolled down to a pristine slice of coast. It was absurd that this was a holiday home, but no self-respecting property portfolio is complete without a few thousand acres of a former colony that you only visit once a year. At the base of the valley, a path of log stepping stones led to a series of thatched huts that resembled an eco lodge, with snack trays of dried mango and a river with a rope swing. Beatriz emerged in a floaty silk beach gown, her mid-morning cocktail in hand.

'Matt!' she beamed. 'Let me introduce you to everyone.'

There were at least twelve family members in total, each with a sillier name than the last. One mother and daughter were called Tam and Taff, though I immediately forgot which was which. Another cousin I was certain introduced herself as Brolly. At the top of the tree were George's parents, Arnold and Phyllis. Beatriz informed me with barely concealed glee that they were divorced and didn't get along. Arnold had a girlfriend thirty years his junior who was *not* welcome at Christmas. Beatriz appeared to view this as a missed opportunity for some drama.

'We're having dinner on the beach tonight,' Beatriz said. 'In your honour.'

There was no evidence to support this claim. Half the family appeared to have already forgotten who I was, and I suspected if pressed would have pegged me as either a friend of the family or a travelling masseur. But I preferred that to feeling like the older brother who held everything together. As we drove down to the beach in a convoy of off-road vehicles, either Tam or Taff looked up and called out 'Giraffes!'

There was a herd of fifteen of them, roaming across the plain as the sun set behind them. I might be jaded as a tutor, but giraffes are giraffes. I got out my phone to take a photo, before realising my enthusiasm was roughly on a par with the eight-year-olds in the group. From there it was a sliding scale of nonchalance, with Arnold about as excited as if we'd spotted some squirrels in Hyde Park. I slid my phone back into my pocket before anyone noticed.

The beach was a spectacular expanse of white sand that stretched as far as the eye could see in both directions. Someone had set up a table and a circle of deckchairs, and Curtis the chef was tending to a barbecue grill. A lesser Kardashian could happily have got married here and been very satisfied with the media content. I wondered how many trips it had taken the staff in the Jeep to make everything look this flawless.

287

As everyone grazed from the barbecue, Beatriz roamed outside the circle, sipping wine while eating nothing. Had this been a reality show, she was the character most liable to start a fight with viral potential, but on today's episode she was happy to prowl ominously. Then the scene took a turn not even a highly creative producer could have scripted. George conferred with the chef then returned to the group, one hand behind his back. 'Here we go,' he said, and held out an egg.

I was going to need some clarification. All the kids were chattering excitedly, but I presumed the intention wasn't to share a raw egg between the twelve of us. Felix explained that this was a family game which involved throwing the egg between your team members while stepping further and further apart. My hair stood on end. I met every cliché pertaining to gay men and ball skills, and had not successfully caught an airborne object since approximately 1994. But it's not like I couldn't claim to have sporting genes. I was, after all, the great-great-grandson of Frederick Knott, who had balanced a county cricket career with his job as a schoolmaster. I was sure I could catch an egg if I put my mind to it.

We split into teams and the game commenced. I quickly relaxed into it. It was scary how fast you could go from feeling like a fly on the wall in a big budget reality show to scoffing at anyone who didn't understand the rules of our beloved egg game. When a family like the Northovers wants you to feel welcome, it's hard to resist their charms. Only too late did I realise the egg was hurtling towards me. It hit me smack on the forehead and splattered all over my face.

Ever since my first meeting with Felix, our lessons had taken place as far as possible from any adult supervision. I always wondered if Beatriz had been eavesdropping that time Felix had thrown a book across the room and had concluded that, like many of her problems, she preferred it out of sight, out of mind. A playroom at the bottom of the garden was already plenty of distance, but here we were sent to the other side of the valley. As we rode over to our designated classroom on quad bikes, we startled a herd of impala drinking at the river delta in the morning light. It was impossible not to be intoxicated by this place, but I was aware of the vast number of staff making things tick behind the scenes. No doubt George felt they were supporting the local economy.

Once installed in our classroom, Felix was full of questions. He had heard me telling his mum about my new boyfriend and demanded to see a photo of the person he referred to as my compadre. It wasn't the absolute fascination with the concept of my personal life that I'd felt at times from Bertie. We were catching up like any old friends. There was no need for any greater sense of urgency, since the Northovers had tacitly accepted that last time they had aimed too high. The school we were now preparing for did not present a challenge academically and I couldn't see Felix failing again. Even so, it was important that if he somehow cocked it up, George had someone to blame.

By day two, our study breaks were the highlight of our daily schedule. This was nothing new for Felix, but our surroundings offered the chance for rather more than a quick round of *Angry Birds*. Lando and Caspian had announced at breakfast that they were heading out in search of baboons, so we decided to see if we could beat them to it. As one of them had commandeered my quad bike, Felix and I were sharing. Felix insisted on being in the driver's seat, and tore off down the valley as I held on desperately. After a few minutes, we came across a herd of zebra.

'Yes!' said Felix, slamming on the accelerator.

'No!' I cried helplessly.

I am unsure what Felix planned to do if he caught up with the zebra. But as he sped forward, we hit a bump. I lost my balance and tumbled backwards.

'Felix!' I called out.

The roar of the engine was too loud. For several seconds, the back of my head bounced merrily along the ground as I clung on and wondered whether I was going to die by being charged down by a herd of zebra or having my skull cracked open by an oblivious child. Eventually Felix heard my shouts and turned to see my feet dangling at his hips.

'Shit!'

He stopped the vehicle. My head was bleeding, but it was nothing serious. We quickly decided the whole thing was hilarious. With the exhilaration that comes from a lucky escape, we narrated what had happened, committing the experience to memory. Then, with a sinking feeling, it was time to go back and study.

'My brain doesn't work at this temperature,' declared Beatriz.

It was an interesting claim from someone who had poured herself a pre-prandial Martini shortly after eleven and been going ever since, but I suppose the heat didn't help. We were alone in the central lodge, which was a perfect opportunity to bitch about George's family. I was ready to blame everything on the patriarchy, but Beatriz was convinced her mother-in-law was the villain. (For this, I blamed the patriarchy.) Phyllis was Dutch and spoke the most extraordinary variety of English, using nouns like quintessence or employing serpentine as a verb. The previous night at dinner, we heard squealing and found one of the dogs mauling a kitten. Everyone froze, alarmed by the kitten's cries. But Phyllis was nonplussed, warding off the dog with a cricket bat then putting the kitten in a bush to die.

'Calm down,' she said to some weeping grandchildren. 'It's not exactly the end of the day.'

A few days into my stay, the family organised a party for New Year's Eve. Someone (I suspected Brolly) had created a table plan which was causing much consternation. Phyllis was upset she had not been seated with Arnold at the head of the table, an arrangement she appeared to favour not for her enjoyment, but as a punishment to him. Perhaps sensing this, Arnold objected furiously to the idea of sitting next to his ex-wife.

Eventually the issue got resolved. Arnold and Phyllis would sit opposite each other, and I — who else? — would go in between. George checked in on me that afternoon to make sure I knew this was a *special* occasion and I ought to wear a collared shirt. He was oddly neutered out here in his parents' company, and I guessed he'd been fighting a losing battle for harmony between them his whole life.

As I took my seat between Arnold and Phyllis that evening, I could barely force a smile. In the wider analysis, my loyalties lay with the spurned wife, but Phyllis didn't inspire you to root for her. I followed Beatriz's example and poured myself a huge glass of wine.

'So,' Arnold said. 'What have you taught Felix?'

It was New Year's Eve, for god's sake. I had no desire to justify my hourly rate. I turned the conversation to small talk. Arnold's only interest was establishing my exact class position so he could treat me accordingly. As I told him where I lived, he pulled a face.

'Shoreditch,' he said. 'That's near Fleet Street.'

'No, Arnold,' Phyllis piped in. 'You are quite wrong.'

Arnold reddened like a pustule.

'Do you live in *town* or not?'

I tried to explain the nature of my neighbourhood by indicting myself as a gentrifier. Arnold drew a sharp intake of breath. My week on the ranch had made it more clear than ever that the system I had upheld as a tutor was as much a hierarchy of race as class. But until now, no one had said the quiet part out loud.

'In our day it was Notting Hill,' Arnold lamented. 'Back then it was nig nog land.'

Felix was granted New Year's Day off. I hadn't planned what to do with myself when there was a knock at the door of my hut. George entered and sat on my bed. It was the kind of impoliteness I had observed among the rich — so careful about manners, only to make these violations which revealed their entitlement.

'I don't suppose you have any plans today, do you?' said George. 'I thought I could give you a tour.'

Leaving the ranch opened my eyes in a way I hadn't managed on my sleep-deprived journey from the airport. It wasn't the first time I had witnessed poverty like this, but it was the first time I had done so in the company of someone so wealthy. People like George set up their lives so they could glide above it — with enough gated compounds and chauffeured transfers, it became easy to ignore. But George was purposefully taking me into the heart of it. As we entered a crowded market, I realised that for him, this was the safari. He insisted on buying me some trinkets to take home, which I hoped the market seller had doubled in price after taking one look at George's designer brogues.

'Now you can sleep well tonight,' George beamed at the seller as he handed over the money.

As we drove off, George told me about Sammy, a caretaker at the ranch. On learning that he could neither read nor write, George had instructed him to attend night school. The question of Sammy's own feelings on the matter, and whether he had the energy for night-time study after a hard day's work, had not entered the equation. Sammy had complied with George's order before dropping out after two months.

'The thing is,' George said, 'he's a simpleton.'

I was fairly sure that wasn't the thing. I was starting to resent being dragged on this excursion — because George wanted a break from his parents? Because he hated his wife and didn't know how to hang out with his children? This was meant to be my day off too. The final stop on our tour was the local beach. It was a municipal strip of sand whose mix of tourists and locals made it a stark contrast to my first night at the ranch. As we looked across the bay, George pointed out the coastline that belonged to his family.

'Six kilometres,' he said proudly.

It's a funny thing, perspective. All of a sudden, I was flush with an anger that had perhaps lurked beneath the surface since the start of my career as a tutor. Maybe it had been there much longer, ever since I had first come into contact with wealth. We are so conditioned to see it as desirable. But private ownership of beaches was illegal in many countries. This one was empty for most of the year, out of bounds to its own citizens so a single family could jet in at Christmas and have it all to themselves. Standing there barefoot on my first night had been magical. Now that I was seeing it in context, it felt obscene.

The following day, George declared that it was time for Felix to shoot his first buck. A ranch hand gave word that the impala were on a part of the plain conducive to being shot at, and a contingent of male relatives rode out on quad bikes as if we were going to war. Unlike on the pheasant shoot, I was rooting for Felix. I didn't find hunting any less strange than I had then, but after the failed entrance test and his family's wider expectations, here was a clean target. Minutes after we approached the herd, Felix took aim and hit a buck first time. As it galloped away in a crazed state, a ranch hand finished it off with a second shot.

The buck fell to the ground and we all gathered round. For a moment, no one knew what to do. The ranch hand started to perform an autopsy, narrating as he went. Lando was very taken with the urine-filled bladder. The ranch hand began warming to his audience, blowing into the buck's windpipe and inflating its lungs like an accordion. We all applauded. Then George stepped forward and daubed blood on Felix's forehead. His position as heir apparent was now official.

I wondered if George was right, and this had all been a big waste of time and money. No wonder it had never felt like teaching. These families didn't want me to expand their child's horizons. It was about treading water, maintaining the status quo, keeping six kilometres of beach in private hands for another generation.

However Felix did in this test, there was no escaping his destiny. They would find a school to take him, and no matter how badly he did there, he would be handed the keys to an empire.

But in another sense, the Northovers had got their money's worth. I had never been invested in our official targets, but I had come to care deeply about Felix's well-being. At times, I had felt like the only person who did. As we went over to our classroom that afternoon, I could tell he didn't have any revision left in him. I asked if he wanted to go looking for baboons.

SPRING TERM 2011

Soraya: I'm really not sure we can afford your leading lady
Me: I thought Anamaria agreed to equity minimum
Soraya: Not her. The chameleon.

Saturday, 22 January, Bethnal Green

Apparently I hadn't got the memo about working with animals and children. After going to meet the chameleon in a reptile shop, I couldn't imagine anyone else in the role. Eventually Soraya found a way to make the budget work. Aside from the cast, everyone was working for free. Soraya had been so successful at securing a crew that we had ended up with a surfeit of runners. I had been assigned my own personal private runner, placing me on equal terms with the chameleon. Soraya may also have been a novice, but she understood instinctively that the only two people who required one-on-one pampering on set were the reptile and the director.

'Spencer,' I said to my personal private runner, hoping I had remembered his name correctly. 'Could you get me a biscuit?'

Soraya rolled her eyes. She had been so worried about the camera equipment that she had spent the previous night sleeping next to it in the flat we had borrowed from a friend for the shoot. I, on the other hand, was standing about six feet from the biscuit table. I had envisaged making some rousing speech to the crew expressing my gratitude. Instead I had tried to project my authority by publicly demanding a Hobnob.

Despite my best efforts, we made it through the day's shooting schedule. The climactic shot was the chameleon darting out her tongue to eat an insect. The handler placed an insect in position, but the chameleon wouldn't bite.

'She can take a while sometimes,' the handler said.

'How long?' Soraya asked anxiously.

'Ooh, can be days.'

Soraya almost had a hernia. But I understood the chameleon. Great art cannot be rushed, and I had finally learned to embrace the meandering path that had led me to this point.

'Let's take five,' I declared. 'Spencer — could you get me a coffee?'

Friday, 4 February, Hackney

I was determined that Fatima would not be a one-off. I got in touch with the teacher who had arranged the interviews at her school and, explaining that I was now a *director,* suggested starting a film club. I had no idea what I meant by the phrase, except that it would be some kind of space where kids could dream and create outside the curriculum. If all went well, I would discover the next Scorsese.

A few weeks later, I woke up and realised I had volunteered to conceive and execute a structured programme for thirty twelve-year-olds. It was not too late to fake an illness, but I found myself turning up at the school and presenting myself to the class in question. I had forgotten how large a class of thirty was. As we waited for latecomers, I observed the class's teacher, Mrs Kilonzo. She was in her fifties and wore a bright woolly jumper and a tired smile. Her command of the room felt like sorcery. She picked out individuals, speaking to some with humour, others with kindness, one or two with unmistakable severity. She was equally attuned to the room's collective energy, knowing the exact moment to quell the class's chatter before it got out of hand.

'Class, I want you to meet Mr Knott.'

I didn't know who she was talking about. Mr Knott was my father's name, a real teacher, an authority figure. But my dad was nowhere in sight. How was I ever going to live up to him? I was a *tutor,* for crying out loud. By my own foolish design I had ended up in charge of a class of pupils, extending a legacy that stretched from Thomas Costen in seventeenth-century Woking to my parents and sister. Not one of them had dropped the baton — not Mildred Knott with her secret lesbian lover, nor Frederick Knott with his professional cricket career. But here I was, the so-called Mr Knott, ready to bring the family profession into permanent disrepute.

'We've got a big treat in store for you today, boys and girls,' Mrs Kilonzo said. The boys and girls looked at their big treat with suspicion. 'Yes, it's our very own Hollywood director!'

I only had myself to blame. The reaction was audible. The kids couldn't believe such a person had walked into their classroom on a Friday afternoon, and they were right. As I introduced myself and they realised the truth of it, their expressions curdled. The fact I had made a short film with a BAFTA-winning actress meant nothing to them, and I could see their respect for me slipping away in real time. All I had left to mention was the YouTube films I had written.

'YouTube? No way!'

A burst of excited chatter rippled across the room. For a pre-teen in 2011, YouTube was the vanguard of audiovisual entertainment, more glamorous and exciting a brand than Cannes or BAFTA could ever hope to be. Mrs Kilonzo cast me a smile, aware that uniting a class's focus like this was nothing to be sniffed at. The question was what to do with it.

Hi Matt,
Still trying to find a date for you to attend a tutor
training session.
Do any of the attached dates work?

Believe it or not, no!

You are a busy man to track down. What about
future months?

My future plans are currently undetermined. I will
let you know when that changes.

Tuesday, 15 February, Mayfair

Philippa had every right to be pissed off. But the more
distance I got from the agency, the better it felt. I had
realised I already had the dream tutoring job. It was the
holding pen. It would be wrong to say it had been there
all along. In the midst of last year's tensions, feeling like
a substitute father for those quasi-orphans had been too
much. But I was in a different place. I decided to set some
ground rules, making clear to Nadia that I was only available for homework help. As long as that was established,
the job suited me. I liked feeling useful as a tutor, but
hated putting pupils under pressure. Both criteria were
satisfied by the absence of parents in the holding pen.

As I turned up that day and waited in the hallway to be assigned a child, I recalled seeing Nick lounging on the stairs that first time. There was no chance of him being there today, given that he had just been nominated for an Olivier Award. I had also heard from a friend of a friend that he was terrible in bed. Actually no, I made that up, but I found it was a good coping mechanism when it came to people whose careers were more advanced than yours.

Nadia sent me upstairs with Roman, the eldest. He was twelve now, which was around the age I started to worry my pupils were going to outpace me.

'Right, what have you got today?'

'French.'

Merde. One of the biggest shocks in moving from the state to the private school system was realising how young they started learning French, and how adept they all were by Roman's age, when I had thought I was sophisticated for knowing the meaning of *syndicat d'initiative*. I had theoretically caught up by taking GCSE and A-Level, but had never lost the feeling that I was behind. I could handle conversation and comprehension at this level, but what put the fear of god in me was being used as a dictionary. Sure enough, ten minutes in Roman turned to me.

'How do you say lobster?'

I paused, fumbling through my memory and wondering what the odds were that the answer was *lobsteur*. Two years ago I would have tied myself in knots, enduring late nights with Rosetta Stone to get myself up to speed. But this wasn't worth the stress. After the lesson, I found Nadia and told her Roman had reached the point of needing a specialist French tutor.

'Fine,' said Nadia. 'Do you know anyone?'

'Yes, actually,' I said. 'My boyfriend.'

Friday, 18 February, Hackney

I decided the best way for Film Club to proceed was by watching some films. This was not in any way influenced by my terror of taking charge of a class of thirty. Getting them to sit in a darkened room for two hours while I did nothing was the best way to stimulate their imaginations. I'd discover the next Scorsese when I was ready.

The first film I chose was *Whale Rider*, about a young Maori girl who wants to be head of her tribe. Despite its faraway setting, I hoped its themes of rebellion and self-determination would prove inspiring. For the first twenty minutes, I was convinced I had failed. The class took the dimming of the lights as a furtive cue, whispering and doing god knows what else out of view. But as the story unfolded, a hush fell. The film's heroine Pai captivated the class with her ambition, only for her to be told that due to her gender, she wasn't allowed to assume her ancestral position.

'Nooooo!' yelled a girl in the front row.

The class laughed.

'Keep it down, Delilah,' said Mrs Kilonzo.

A few scenes later, Pai met with further resistance. 'Girls aren't allowed,' her father informed her categorically.

'What the *hell*?' said Delilah.

Her classmates laughed again.

'She loves an audience, this one,' Mrs Kilonzo tutted.

I didn't doubt it. But the fact she was compelled to perform her responses only made them more sincere. I no longer felt nervous about our impending shift to practical filmmaking. I had been worried the class might turn shy when asked to appear on camera. Now I knew we had a star in our midst.

Monday, 21 February, Mayfair

It had been a while since I had fretted about coming out to a client. But introducing a boyfriend to the workplace was another matter. Being gay was an abstract concept compared to the physical reality of the person you had sex with. Nadia had barely reacted when I suggested Julien, and I worried this meant it was an issue. But the next time I saw her she was full of questions and started talking merrily about her husband and his half-hearted attempts to learn Arabic.

'Fucking hell!' said Julien after his first lesson. 'That house is weird.'

It felt good to know that someone saw it as I did. But Julien couldn't believe I had been happy to leave the whereabouts of the boys' parents a mystery. I hadn't realised I was dating Miss Marple, but after piecing together some information gleaned from the house with a couple of Google searches, Julien called me excitedly.

'Oh my god. You're not going to believe who their parents are!'

It turned out that the boys' father was an extremely wealthy businessman who had got in trouble with the law. There had been headlines and repercussions, and it appeared that the decision to educate the boys in a different country was not a purely educational one. It wasn't their fault their father was a crook, and I imagined the whole experience had been fairly traumatic. But I wasn't convinced it justified being on the family payroll.

I would be lying if I said I didn't let the revelation affect my relationship with the boys. Now that I knew what they had endured, they didn't want a tutor who pretended their homework held any more meaning than it did.

'Do you know the chemical symbol for sodium?' Samir asked.

I paused for a moment.

'No.'

It would have taken one of us a matter of seconds to look it up. But after a mutual glance, which contained perhaps the greatest level of understanding that ever passed between us, Samir left the answer blank.

Zoe: How's the edit going?

Me: Almost there! Can't wait for Sunday

Sunday, 6 March, Hackney Wick

As soon as we had a cut of the film, we started submitting it to festivals. I was convinced we were going to get into Venice and win a Golden Lion, but perhaps sensing that this was a long shot, Soraya arranged a cast and crew screening underneath a motorway flyover in Hackney. Far from being a dud location, it was a space that had been reclaimed by a team of young architects and an intimidatingly cool place for our film to screen. Email invites were despatched and my parents drove up from Dorset. The moment the film began to play, I felt sick.

'It's the wrong aspect ratio!' I shouted.

'No it's not,' Soraya said calmly.

I looked back at the picture in confusion. *Something felt wrong.* But it wasn't the aspect ratio — it was seeing my work on screen. How could it not be disappointing? My other screenplays might never have been made, but they had always been rich in that most alluring of qualities — potential. This was a finished product, and its flaws were there for all to see.

'We're very proud of you,' said my mum afterwards, which is the only review any artist ever wants.

'You made a film!' said another friend.

Zoe ran up and gave me a hug. There would be time for honest feedback, but she knew what I needed today. I told her about the comment the friend had made, suggesting that it was a neat way to avoid giving any criticism.

'Who cares?' said Zoe. 'It's true.'

She was right. I wasn't going to win a Golden Lion. I wasn't even sure I had anything much to say yet. But after so many hours sitting in front of a laptop dreaming up images, I finally had something to show.

'Shit,' I said. 'I made a film.'

Friday, 11 March, Hackney

I had introduced the practical element of Film Club as a purposefully dull lecture series, my goal not to educate but fool Mrs Kilonzo into thinking I was capable of class control. For several weeks now, I had strung out my explanation of what amounted to pressing stop and start on a camera phone, a skill in which the class were already universally accomplished. Perhaps for that reason, I could feel them growing restless. The time had come to let my fledging cineastes run riot.

They divided into groups of four or five, but those assigned to work with Delilah understood that they were in the presence of an auteur. I had given the groups a selection of titles to choose from — largely to torpedo the plans of a boy who was hell-bent on making a film about a vomiting dog — and Delilah had gone for the title 'Last Day On Earth', scripting a story based on her own original idea for herself to star in. She was a girl after my own heart.

'Action!' Delilah shouted from behind the classroom door. It was not a command traditionally given by the lead actor, but the designated director saw no sense in trying to contain the talent. Delilah came bursting into the room, having back-combed her hair and used eyeliner to scrawl on an inch-thick pair of eyebrows and a moustache. She was hooting and screaming in a language of unknown origin, which is not to say it felt in any way illogical when she burst into an a cappella rendition of the Thong Song. Her classmates, who had been cast as her classmates, reacted with bemusement. It was how they reacted to her every day, but Delilah had conceived a narrative in which her outsized gestures were not the joke but a legitimate response to an impending apocalypse, and her classmates' nonchalance for once the punchline. It was an ingenious concept, allowing her to unleash both her tremendous need for self-expression and her bafflement that no one appeared to share this urge. But its true brilliance was in its understanding of the form, for while Delilah's wild energy was cause for criticism and derision in her daily life, on film it was the opposite. The camera lives for such charisma, and it was clear to all present that we were capturing a thrilling performance.

'This is going to be so good,' I said to Delilah.

'Am I going to win an Oscar?'

It was fair to say that for her role in 'Last Day On Earth', Delilah was not one of the frontrunners for the following year's Academy Awards. But who was I to tell someone who shared my aspirations to settle for an achievable goal rather than battle improbable odds? The more time I spent in a school like this, the more guilty I felt about how I had chosen to spend the past two and a half years. Once you were in a room with a child, you were inclined to give them the time of day. But time is a finite resource. It was teachers like Mrs Kilonzo who deserved the praise, when I had put all my energy into giving a leg-up to pupils who didn't really need it.

I don't want to give myself too much credit. No matter how I chose to divide my attention, the children of the elite were destined to glide to the top of society while the Delilahs of the world would come up against obstacles again and again. If I had been any use to anyone, it was in the moment — stepping into the gaps that arose between teachers, parents and friends to provide bursts of encouragement, inspiration or company. So many of those moments would fade from my pupils' memory, some almost instantly. But there was no knowing which ones would resonate.

'Definitely,' I said to Delilah. 'Better start preparing your speech.'

Beatriz: Matt!!! He got in!!!!!!!!!!!!!!

Tuesday, 15 March, Highgate

It was the result I had expected. But after all this time, I couldn't quite believe it was real. Apparently nor could Beatriz, since minutes after texting she called me to revel in the news. Once she was on the phone, she insisted I come for a visit. A few days later, I hauled myself up to Highgate at the oddly specific time of 4.40 p.m. to be greeted by a smiling Beatriz.

'Matt!' she said, embracing me warmly. 'Let's celebrate.'

I was expecting her to crack open a bottle of their finest vintage Moët, but apparently she had something else in mind. Entering the living room, I saw that it was not Felix but George who had found me five minutes.

Were we finally going to have that threesome? I had never lost my hatred of these enforced bonding sessions with parents. Felix might have got to see a bit of the real me, but with Beatriz and George it had never stopped being a performance.

'We actually wanted to talk to you about something,' said Beatriz. 'George is making a few changes. We're going to be based in Hampshire from next year.'

I knew immediately what she was asking.

'You'd have your own cottage on the estate. And car.'

Beatriz began listing the other perks of the job, from frequent holidays to unlimited access to their personal chef. All these luxuries to which I had occasionally been treated could now be mine on a regular basis. It was impossible not to be tempted. But that was as far as it went.

'I don't think that's going to be possible,' I said awkwardly.

Beatriz looked surprised. So did George. They weren't used to people saying no, especially not staff. For a moment, I worried they were going to make me an offer I couldn't refuse. But George just got up and left.

'Right,' said Beatriz, all her warmth vanished. 'I guess this is it then. Thanks for everything, Matt.'

You'd think she could have kept up the act a few seconds longer. But Beatriz had never hidden the fact that our friendship was conditional. As she showed me towards the door a little too eagerly, I reminded her I hadn't seen Felix.

'Oh yes,' said Beatriz. 'He's in the cinema.'

This had long since lost its novelty, but I still got a pang of sympathy every time I walked in and saw Felix sunk into a bean bag, half-watching some Pixar film. He didn't react as I entered. I hated goodbyes at the best of times, and had no idea how I was going to access the appropriate sentiment with an eleven-year-old boy.

'Well done for getting in!'

Felix looked up sceptically.

'Did I get in because my dad paid for a new sports centre?'

Of *course* George had. What bothered me was not the fact that he had made some big donation, but that Felix had been made aware of it. It was a question

311

that would always niggle at him, no matter what I said. I had a horrible vision of Felix walking past this glistening new edifice every day of his school career and being taunted by the thought that he was only there thanks to his father's intervention, rather than anything he had achieved.

'No,' I said. 'Definitely not. You earned it.'

I'm not sure either of us bought what I was saying. As ever with Felix, it was hard to know if my efforts would have any impact on the greater forces at play in his life. But at least I could say I'd tried.

'This might be the last time I see you,' I said.

I had no idea if his parents had told him about the job offer. Whatever his thoughts, Felix felt no need to share them.

'I can't believe it's been more than two years,' I persisted. 'Do you remember our first lesson?'

Felix took a long look at me.

'I remember how bad you were at skiing.'

'Oh god,' I said. 'I was really terrible.'

'Seriously,' said Felix, grinning. 'So shit.'

ACKNOWLEDGEMENTS

Thank you to my editor Jamie Coleman for seeing the best version of this book long before I did, steering me when I needed it and trusting me when I didn't. Nothing feels better than hearing you have been reading your favourite lines to your wife in the kitchen. To my agent Cathryn Summerhayes for containing my anxieties and demanding more sex scenes; Clarissa Sutherland for flawlessly guiding me to the finish line; Fola Adebayo, Ellen Turner, Jess Molloy, Linden Lawson, Mafruhdha Miah, Shyam Kumar, Steve Marking, Yadira Da Trindade and everyone else at Trapeze, Orion and Curtis Brown for your endless patience and enthusiasm.

To everyone who taught me how to write or encouraged me, especially John James, Frank Ahern, Caroline Barrett and, most of all, Stephen Davies, for understanding how much some goats need herding. To Allegra Huston for honesty before I knew I needed it; Victoria Grew and Joe Scantlebury for honing my jokes in another medium; Cynthia Okoye for believing in me from the beginning; Erica Segre for describing this book as the perfect betrayal and every other inimitable turn of phrase. I'm sorry you'll never get to read this.

To my friends — Amia Srinivasan for pitch perfect notes and even better snack plates; Amrou Al-Kadhi for the wild ride we've been on and lifting me up in good times and bad; Daniel Chandler for so much love and support and all the ways we have grown together; Farhana Bhula for being the Agustin to my Pedro; Georgia Beaufort for never separating fun and kindness; Georgie Fozard for convincing me my future was bright; Grace Chatto for staying so thoughtful amid so many fun times; Hermione Hoby for reading like a true friend; Peter Knegt for a love that runs deep and a lifetime of adventures; Toby Ashraf for asking the right questions and being funnier than anyone; Jack Patterson, Bea Philips and Simon Amstell for being the best things about North London; Max Colson, Emily Craig and Jess Wear for keeping my heart in South London; Ruth, Ricky, Camilla, Guido, Jess and Saul for acting like semi-professionals and not being fucking idiots; Dylan for being part of the story; Cindy for being family; Nicki & Simon and Jane & Phil for being there when I needed it; Eric, Yahia, Bettina and Trevor for being miles away but feeling like home.

To Vincent Chabany-Douarre for invaluable input at the eleventh hour, the dankest hot takes imaginable and giving me new perspective on everything.

To my aunts and uncles, Simon & Elaine and Annie & Jeremy, and my godparents Griselda, Colin and Jonathan,

ACKNOWLEDGEMENTS

for treating me like a grown-up long before I deserved it; my siblings Jonny, Chris and Lizzy for being the genesis of my sense of humour and teaching me to share the stage gracefully; Emma for making the arguably insane move of becoming a Knott by choice and Freddie for having no choice in the matter; my dad Richard for building me a puppet theatre when I was seven and quietly applauding every story I've told since; my mum Tricia for playing Monty Python tapes in the car and every other way you made a nest for your babies.

Finally to Sophie Smith — this book was your idea and is full of your voice and your thoughts. But nothing I write here feels sufficient. I can't imagine who or where I'd be without the past seventeen years of your love, generosity and script notes. I'm never not looking forward to our next margarita.

CREDITS

Trapeze would like to thank everyone at Orion who worked on the publication of *A Class of Their Own*.

Agent
Cathryn Summerhayes

Editor
Jamie Coleman

Copy-editor
Linden Lawson

Proofreader
Ian Greensill

Editorial Management
Clarissa Sutherland
Carina Bryan
Jane Hughes

Charlie Panayiotou
Tamara Morriss
Claire Boyle

Audio
Paul Stark
Jake Alderson
Georgina Cutler

Contracts
Anne Goddard
Ellie Bowker
Humayra Ahmed

Design
Nick Shah

Steve Marking
Joanna Ridley
Helen Ewing

Finance
Nick Gibson
Jasdip Nandra
Elizabeth Beaumont
Ibukun Ademefun
Afeera Ahmed
Sue Baker
Tom Costello

Inventory
Jo Jacobs
Dan Stevens

Marketing
Folayemi Adebayo
Yadira Da Trindade

Production
Katie Horrocks
Fiona McIntosh

Publicity
Ellen Turner

Sales
Jen Wilson
Victoria Laws
Esther Waters
Frances Doyle
Ben Goddard
Jack Hallam
Anna Egelstaff
Inês Figueira
Barbara Ronan
Andrew Hally
Dominic Smith
Deborah Deyong
Lauren Buck
Maggy Park
Linda McGregor
Sinead White
Jemimah James
Rachael Jones
Jack Dennison
Nigel Andrews
Ian Williamson
Julia Benson
Declan Kyle
Robert Mackenzie
Megan Smith
Charlotte Clay
Rebecca Cobbold